James E. Thorold (James Edwin Thorold) Rogers

Social Economy

James E. Thorold (James Edwin Thorold) Rogers

Social Economy

ISBN/EAN: 9783744644983

Printed in Europe, USA, Canada, Australia, Japan

Cover: Foto ©Suzi / pixelio.de

More available books at **www.hansebooks.com**

SOCIAL ECONOMY

BY

J. E. THOROLD ROGERS

TOOKE PROFESSOR OF ECONOMIC SCIENCE, UNIVERSITY OF OXFORD

REVISED FOR AMERICAN READERS

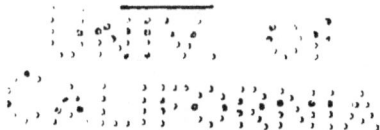

NEW YORK & LONDON

G. P. PUTNAM'S SONS

The Knickerbocker Press

1893

PREFACE.

THE object of this little book is to give instruction in the rudiments of social science, and to do so in such language and in such a form as will make the subject clear to the youngest students. The author has stated what he has to say in the shape of a series of lessons, each of which should be carefully read and understood before the pupil passes on to the next. It is hoped that when he has read through the whole, he will have got some insight into the laws which regulate social life.

It does not follow that knowledge will make the person who possesses it discreet and wise; but no person will be discreet and wise without knowledge. After that training which is necessary for each person in order that he may earn his living, no knowledge can be more usefully turned to account than that which explains the circumstances under which men live together in a civilized society, and confer benefits on each other. It is this knowledge which the author hopes to have given in the following pages.

OXFORD, Dec. 1, 1871.

225387

PREFACE TO THE AMERICAN EDITION

In preparing this volume for American Students, I have made no changes in the original plan, and have not pretended to add any thing to the clear and satisfactory text of the author. I have merely translated his references to currency, measurements, trades, etc., from the English to the American terms, and changed some of the more important illustrations, so as to make them apply to American circumstances. I do not of course suppose that the American boy who will read this volume, does not understand what is meant by a pound sterling, or a stone weight, but as the lesson to be taught is one of principles, and not of comparative values, I think the changes I have made will save him from giving time to any unnecessary details.

The spirit and purpose of the book are excellent, and its teachings combine to a rare degree, simplicity and thoroughness. A full understanding of the principles it explains, will give to our young American students the basis of the knowledge that is indispensable for the clear-headed citizens and wise legislators, they should aim to become.

G. H. F.

June, 1872.

CONTENTS.

1*

CONTENTS.

CONTENTS.

SOCIAL ECONOMY.

LESSON I.

SAVAGE AND CIVILIZED LIFE.

FEW of the readers of this book have not seen a town, and most of them have probably lived in or visited the larger towns or cities.

But nearly all American boys and girls will know that a little more than two centuries ago, there were not any cities or towns on this continent, and the people who lived on it, the Indians, wandered about the country, chasing the wild animals, or fishing, or digging roots, in order to get food.

In other countries, such as England, France, or Germany, the time when there were no towns was a good deal further back, but in them also some centuries ago, people had to get their living by hunting or fishing, or by pasturing such flocks and herds as they possessed wherever they could find grass for them to live upon.

In those old days the people who could get their living in a country like England for instance, by the chase or by pasturing cattle, were very few, not more indeed than could be reckoned in a middle-sized town at the present day. Few as they were, they were all that could live. If the summer was very dry, or the spring very

backward, many were starved. The whole of England
and Wales in those ancient times did not maintain a
hundredth part of the number who live in it at present,
and did not maintain this hundredth part as securely and
as comfortably as every Englishman is maintained now.
There are parts of the world where the inhabitants live
just as our forefathers lived in England ages ago, such as
the Indian territories of the United States, the greater
part of Africa, and large tracts in Asia.

The inhabitants of these scantily settled and unculti-
vated countries are said to be savages. Those who live
in countries settled and civilized like our own are said
to be civilized. The savage is poor, ignorant, and lives
from day to day. The civilized man is, in comparison at least, rich, wise, and has made some provision
for the future. What are the causes which make so
great a difference between the condition of the savage
and that of the civilized man?

I purpose in this little book to give an account of
some among the causes which make this mighty difference. I cannot give them all, for if I tried to do so
the book would not be little, and what is perhaps more
to the purpose, I should mix up things which had better
be kept separate. For example, good and just laws,
wise and fair government on the part of rulers, virtuous
and honest action on the part of subjects, are powerful
causes of civilization. But I am not writing a book
about law, or government, or moral conduct: I shall
only try to show what is the reason why a hundred civilized people can live on the space of ground which will
hardly keep one savage alive; why it is civilized people
can live together in great towns, and are the better for
their neighbors, while a savage man is anxious to have as

few neighbors near him as possible. Stated in a very few words, the savage is obliged to do every thing for himself, and the civilized man is able to get an infinite number of things done for him.

The principal necessaries of life are food, clothing, lodging. If we add to these the means of moving from place to place, we shall find that most labor is given with a view to satisfying those wants, either immediately or indirectly. For example, a farmer who sows a field with wheat is immediately engaged in the supply of food, while the smith who constructs a plough is indirectly concerned with the same service. There is the same difference between one who shears wool, or grows cotton, and another who makes the weaving machine wherewith to spin either substance into cloth.

The savage man has to provide himself with food, and with the implements or weapons necessary to obtain food, to make himself clothing, and to manufacture the tools needed for piecing the skins together which he wears. But the civilized man gets his fellow-man to do a vast number of these services for him, and does some service himself, in return for which he is able to get such conveniences as he requires. And he gets what he needs more regularly, more easily, more plentifully, and more cheaply than he would if he lived a savage life.

As the civilized man gets what he wants more cheaply than a savage does, so he gets it more regularly. A great city like New York depends for its food, for the materials of the clothes which its inhabitants wear, and of the houses in which they live, on other regions. It is, so to speak, wholly dependent on other places for all which its inhabitants need. But it gets them regularly—with the exactness and precision, as people say, of clockwork. The case is very different with those who live a savage life, or even with those who are only partly civilized. Such people are liable to sudden ca lamities. A famine comes, and half the people perish . sickness overtakes them, and the same result ensues.

Again, you will see people going out to their work —engaged in the business of their shops and counting houses—occupied in a number of different industries They are eager in carrying on their calling, and have no anxiety, except as to the best way to do that which lies before them. But in countries where men do not understand the laws which are needful for the security of society, violence breeds suspicion and fear, and men are hindered in their calling by the necessity of defending themselves.

It is plain, then, that there are conditions of human life where men are unskilful; where the means of life are irregular; where labor, unless the workman carries arms and is suspicious and watchful, is wholly unsafe. Now the discovery of the means by which the largest number of persons can live in the greatest plenty, can look forward to the greatest regularity, and can do their work in the greatest safety, is the object of what is called "social science."

LESSON II.

A LOAF OF BREAD.

IF you take a loaf of bread, and think of the persons who are set to work in order to produce or supply that loaf, you will find that the number of such persons is very large. The three principal persons are the farmer, the miller, and the baker. But the farmer almost always employs labor, both of man and beast, in order to get his crop in. He also uses implements which are made by the labor of the carpenter, the smith, and in our time by the machinist, for the employment of finished machines in husbandry is becoming very common. The presence of the smith calls into activity the work of those who raise iron and coal. Another kind of skill is needed in order to work iron and coal profitably—to direct the labor of those who are engaged in those industries.

Again, the miller requires the service of those who quarry to supply him with the best stones with which to grind his flour—that of the weaver to supply him with the cloth, or of the worker in metals, who manufactures the metal sieve through which the flour is sifted, and of another kind of weaver who makes the sack in which both corn and flour are stored. The mill in which he carries on his work is the product of another set of laborers—the carpenter, the joiner, the wheelwright, the mason, the brick-

layer.   If the power which he employs is water, a special
kind of skill is needed in order to use the force of run-
ning or falling water; if it be wind, he will want the services of the weaver of such cloth as catches the wind;
if it be steam, a still more numerous and more scientific
class of workmen must be employed.

The baker, again, needs his assistants before he can
carry on his calling.   If he prepares his bread in wooden
vessels, he calls in the help of the cooper.   The brick-
maker or quarryman supplies the bricks or stones of which
his oven is built; or in case the oven be made of iron, the
miner and the smith must work to get the materials and
fashion them.   If the bread be baked in some shape or
mould, other kinds of labor are needed.   If it be made
by machinery—as the best bread is now made—another
set of persons is called on to exercise their industry.   If
the baker weighs his bread before he sells it—as he is
bound to do—another set of persons supplies the weights
and scales; and so on with the materials of which those
implements are made.

For reasons which will be given further on, it is not
found possible to carry out their transactions without
money.   Money is made of metals, which are, for the most
part, discovered and worked in distant and barren regions.   Here, then, is another field of labor.   The miner
is supported by food and other necessaries, which are carried to him in ships.   The building of a ship calls into activity a whole host of industries, many of which the experience or knowledge of my readers will remind them
of.   When the gold and silver are brought to this country,
other people must be set to work, in order that the met
als may be refined, cut into pieces, and stamped as coins
and a very nice and delicate process the work of coining is

Now I have only named a few of those persons who are engaged in producing a very simple necessary of life.

But besides those who labor mostly with their hands, there is another class of men who labor mostly with their heads—the class of employers or, as they are sometimes called, capitalists. These men are engaged in directing the labor of others, or in studying the market, and in keeping up a continual supply of goods at as steady a price as possible. Unless persons were found to devote themselves to trade, the advantage of a steady, regular supply of the necessaries and conveniences of life would not be forthcoming.

I said above that a savage was ignorant. He is a savage because he is ignorant. It would be impossible to keep the advantages of civilization unless each successive generation were taught. If any society of men were to resolve not to give any instruction to their children—not to communicate to their descendants what they know themselves, such a society would in a short time relapse into the condition of savages. Nations are civilized because they inherit the knowledge as well as the property of their ancestors. Some of this knowledge is imparted by the skilled workman, either with or without the formality of apprenticeship; but a great deal of the knowledge is given by the schoolmaster, who therefore discharges a most important duty to future society.

There are, then, a very large number of persons engaged in producing and supplying a loaf of bread.

Perhaps my readers will wish to know why it is that I have chosen a loaf of bread in order to illustrate the great fact, that a civilized society is united by the mutual services which its several members render to each other.

I began by stating that the same space of earth could maintain a hundred times more civilized people than it could savages; in other words, it produces a hundred times more food besides producing it with far greater regularity. The number of people who can live in any country or in any town is measured by the number of loaves which this people can produce or can purchase. If the whole of America were as densely peopled as New York is, it would not contain too many persons, provided those who lived in it could procure necessary sustenance. There is, then, a great deal to be learnt from a loaf of bread.

EVERY one of the persons who assists in supplying a loaf of bread is paid out of the price of the loaf. The portion which some of these persons receive is, no doubt, excessively small, but still it is received. The price is said to be *distributed* among the several persons who *contribute* towards the loaf. A portion of the price, however, is paid to one person who does not contribute any thing; this is the person who owns the land. It must not be supposed that he has no right to get it; it is impossible to prevent his having it. If any other person—whether it be the community at large or the farmer who occupies the land—were to take this portion, it would only mean that the community made itself the landowner, or that the farmer was turned into a landowner.

Let us see how this comes to pass. We shall be able to discover it more easily, if we take the case of some country which is differently situated from our own.

However valuable, useful, or even necessary a thing may be, it bears no price if every person can get as much as he pleases of it without any trouble. Without air we could not live two minutes; but, as under ordinary circumstances, everybody can get as much air as he likes, he need pay nothing for it. So with water, though in less degree. In the United States, and in the country parts of Europe, water bears no price, because it can easily be had for the getting; but in the great towns of Europe, especially in such a town as London, water does bear a price, though the price is so low for those who want to drink it, that no one but a churl would think he did you any great favor in giving you a glass of water.

Now let us take the case of the middle island in the New Zealand group. The first settlers in that island found a few savages there, but only a few. The climate of the island is very like that of England, and the land is as fit for ordinary crops as that of our own country. Much, no doubt, was covered by wood, but there was abundance of open ground.

As any person who came thither could have as much land as he wished, land was worth nothing; and no bit of land was more desirable than any other bit, or the most desirable bits were far in excess of the wants of the colonists. But in course of time a change occurs. Some bits get to be more desirable than others. The first place in which such a change takes place is in the towns. A road is made, and a place near the road is worth more than a place further from it. The town is a seaport, and the land near the sea is worth more than that which is more distant. A market is set up, and a plot near the market is more desirable than one which is less convenient. Immediately on such occasions, the land which is thus favored yields more advantages than other land does or, in other words, begins to yield a rent.

In all newly-settled countries rent arises first in the

towns, since the causes which make rent begin here first. In course of time the influence of this cause is rendered wider. The agricultural land near the town begins to be worth more than that which is further off It may not grow more corn, but it costs less to bring what it grows to market. It may have no greater natural fertility, but it is at a shorter distance from the place whence it can get the means of artificial fertility. The occupier of such land finds an easier market for his produce. He is put to less cost in carrying manures to his farm, and conveying machinery thither. If he tried to sell his farm, he could get a price for it, which would be beyond the value of what he has laid out on it; and the fact that he could get such a price shows that it is paying a rent.

By-and-by other farms, as the people get more numerous, begin to share in these advantages. It does not follow that farm produce gets a penny dearer; it may even get cheaper. It very often happens, in countries such as I have described, that while land yields no rent whatever, the produce of land is exceedingly dear. In other words, the prices of wheat, butter, wool, and a host of other things, have nothing whatever to do with the rent of land.

In the end, all the land of the country which can return any produce to labor is occupied. It is still the business of the farmer to turn his land to the best advantage, and as he does so, the owner of the land shares in the advantage of the farmer's skill. So the shopkeeper tries, in so far as the place where he carries on his business will aid him, to get the greatest advantage out of his shop; and if the advantage does depend on the situation of his shop, his landlord will share the

gain. If his landlord did not share it, the occupier
would keep it to himself. But being better off than his
neighbor is, by the possession of this advantage of situation, he would be able to sell his advantage—that is to
say, he would become a landowner.

Now this is the way in which rent arises. Nor is
there any limit to its increase, as long as the intelligence
of men is devoted towards improving husbandry, and
the number of people who live on farm produce in-
creases with these improvements. In such a country as
England land has become exceedingly valuable, partly
because agriculture is practised so well in it, partly
because the trade of the country has so mightily increased, and therefore people are willing to give so
much for the right of occupying land which lies advan-
tageously for trade.

The owner of land therefore gets a share in that
which labor produces without having contributed to
that labor. But he does not get it by violence or
wrong; it comes to him by a law of nature, since whatever is scarce and useful will fetch a price. Now when
land is fully settled it begins to be scarce, and as in order for man to live he must get food by husbandry,
there can be nothing more useful than that which supplies the means of life.

LESSON IV.

THE SHARE OF THE WORKMAN.

I HAVE shown you how it is that the owner of land gets a portion of the price at which the loaf is sold : the rest of the price is divided among those who work.

To work means to use one's bodily powers or one's powers of mind. Of course no one can use his bodily strength to a purpose, in any calling whatever, unless he brings his mind to bear on his work; nor can the cleverest and quickest thinker dispense with some bodily effort. When, therefore, we say that one man's labor is bodily and another's is mental, we merely mean that the work is more of the body in the one case, and more of the mind in the other. Useful qualities of mind are rarer than useful qualities of body, and are therefore more costly. The manager of a business is better paid than a common workman is, because his skill is scarcer. A great lawyer or a wise physician is more highly paid than a person of ordinary abilities in either of those callings is, because great powers in each of those professions are rare, and the service which each of those persons renders is very much sought after. There is a sort of fertility of men's minds very like the fertility of certain fields. In places where wine is grown, one spot of land will produce wine fifty times as valuable as that

which comes from another spot, which to all appearance
is of just the same quality; so the work of one man may
be paid for at fifty times the rate at which another man's
work is paid, simply because people find out that it is
worth fifty times as much.

It is common to say that such and such a person
has put so much *money* or *capital* into a workshop or
business. This only means that he has put so much
work into it, though the work is shown in different ways
and under different shapes. I will try to make this clear
to you.

With one exception, and I have explained this exception in the last lesson, every thing valuable gets its
worth because work is expended on it. If the workman has given his work wisely, the price of what he sells
agrees with the pains he has been at to produce that
which he sells. If he makes that which nobody wants,
he will have wasted his labor altogether. If he makes
more than is wanted, he will have wasted some of his
labor. If he takes more time to make it than other
people do, he will give more work for less price than
other workmen do. Now everybody wishes to get as
much as he can for his work, and to work as little as he
can for what he gets.

These are very plain facts, but they have been the
causes which have led to that result of which I spoke at
first—that in the present day a hundred persons can get
their living where some centuries ago hardly one person
could live.

The reason why a piece of gold, roughly speaking, is
worth fifteen times as much as a piece of silver of the
same weight, and twelve hundred times as much as a
piece of copper of the same weight, is that on the whole

it takes fifteen and twelve hundred times as much work to get a pound of gold as it does the same weights of silver and copper.

The reason why one house in a street is worth a thousand dollars, and another house in the same street is worth two thousand, is that the second cost twice as much to build as the other did.

The reason why a hundredweight of wheat is generally worth half as much again as a hundredweight of barley, is the fact that it generally costs half as much more labor or expense to grow the former than it does to grow the latter.

The reason why one kind of manual labor is worth twenty-five cents a day, and another kind is worth a dollar, is because it has cost so much more to prepare the latter kind of workman than it has to bring up the former.

In brief, the value or price of any thing, whether it be work done or labor to be hired, agrees with the cost of making the thing or preparing the laborer.

Nobody who wishes to get his living by any calling betakes himself to making that which nobody wants. It would be waste of labor to make parlor grates in a tropical climate, or sun-blinds in an arctic one. It is true that many people get their living by making or supplying things which others would be far better without; but there are many things which people wish for, and sacrifice a great deal for, though their use is mischievous or even ruinous.

Again, if more of any article is made than is generally wanted, some of the labor is wasted. It sometimes happens that more cotton or woollen cloth is made than people want to buy. But this evil soon rights itself.

The commonest and worst case is when too many people enter into any calling. Thus it is said that at present there are more tailors and shoemakers than are needed to make clothes and shoes. Unfortunately, there have been for many a year too many needle-women. Now when too many people are engaged in any calling, they will either get low wages or irregular employment. It is as plain as figures can show that if there be only work for three, and six seek work, there are only two courses open for them: either the six must work so cheaply as to induce employers to give them full work, or each must work half-time.

Lastly, the workman may take too much time at his work. He may be idle, or unskilful, or weak, may have bad tools, or not possess improved tools. In working land a plough is better than a spade, a steam cultivator better than a plough. In spinning yarn a hand-wheel is better than a spindle, a spinning-jenny better than a hand-wheel. An ill-fed workman is less profitable than a well-fed one, often even if the latter is paid double the former's wages, for low wages is very often another name for dear labor.

LESSON V.

THE COURSE OF IMPROVEMENT.

In the last lesson it was stated that everybody wishes to get as much as he can for his work, and to work as little as he can for what he gets. When I say that he wishes to work as little as he can, I don't mean that he wishes to turn out an inferior article, but that he wants to supply an article equally good with that which his neighbor supplies, but at less cost to himself.

There is nothing which has helped the progress of mankind more than this motive or impulse. It has caused every kind of improvement in the manufacture of useful things. It has led men, with greater or less success, to devote themselves to that calling for which they find themselves most fitted. In seeking their own good they have done the best service to their fellow-men.

I cannot illustrate what I have said better than by referring to the progress of agriculture. Two or three centuries ago the art of the farmer was very rude. He reaped a very scanty return for his seed; he knew nothing about those roots on which cattle are maintained in the winter-time, and his stock of animals was coarse and lean. But he was as diligent and thrifty in his calling as he now is. He paid rent, and got his living by his work on the farm.

The first discovery he made was the value of turnips and carrots. Before he found out the use of these roots he had only a little coarse hay to feed his cattle on in the winter. In consequence, towards autumn it used to be the custom to kill all the animals who could not be kept through the winter, and the people lived on salted provisions for several months. Now he is able to keep his stock, and get fresh meat all the year round. But the more animals that can be kept on a farm, the more grain can be grown; and the increase of live stock led to an increase in the yield of corn. Next—always with the same motive, to get the greatest return at the least possible cost—the farmer began to think what were the best kinds of grass on which to feed his stock, and which could be made into hay. Thus he sowed clover and rye grass, and other so-called grasses. More feed and more stock followed. By-and-by he began to choose his stock of cattle and sheep. He found that some breeds yielded more profit than others, and he selected these for his farm. Then he studied the land which he tilled, and found that draining would better this field, and chalk would better that. Then he learned the use of artificial manures, as certain substances are called. Lastly—always with the same motive—he began to use better and more powerful instruments for stirring the ground, for reaping or mowing the produce, and for threshing the seed.

The end of all this has been that the land yields five times as much produce as it did in the days before these discoveries were made. The motive for these discoveries was the expectation of greater profit on labor—*i.e.*, the farmer's own interest. This he furthered in the first instance. But the nation at large had its advantage in greater plenty, in more regular supply, and therefore in the means for maintaining a large number of persons. The landowner got his advantage in the increase of his rent, which kept growing, for the reasons given in the last lesson but one.

The same results have occurred in manufactures. The inhabitants of any country must live on its produce, or be able, in case they are too numerous for the land of the country to maintain them, to get the produce of other countries in exchange for what they make. Now it is clear, if agriculture is so backward that everybody's time is occupied in tilling the land, while the produce is only just sufficient to keep alive those who are engaged in tillage, that nobody can betake himself to any other calling. And conversely, if the art of agriculture is so advanced that a fifth part of the people can produce the food which is required for all, four-fifths of the people may be employed in some other calling, and many of these, under certain circumstances, need do no work at all.

Now the manufacturer is open to the same influence which moves the farmer. He makes cloth, for example.

If he can lessen his own cost or labor he will get a greater return for his labor; so he eagerly welcomes all machines which shorten labor or lessen cost. Part of this extra advantage he keeps for himself, part he bestows on the public by lessening the price of that which he makes. At the present time it is probable that it does not take a fiftieth part of the time and trouble to make a yard of cloth that it did in the days when farmers began to improve agriculture. Meanwhile the people at large have got better and cheaper clothing.

When we think of the conditions under which the

industry of any society of men is carried on, we shal.
constantly discover that while men are endeavoring, by
just and lawful means—that is, without violence, unfairness, or dishonesty—to further their own interests, they
always further the interests of others also; and the reason why this always takes place is that they who are engaged in honest industry are trying to do their neighbors
a service.   It is true that they expect some other service
in return; but the exchange of these services is a mutual
advantage.   If I have made a pair of boots, and my neighbor has made a table, and we agree to exchange these two
useful articles, the fact of our making the exchange means
that I prefer the table to the boots, and he prefers the
boots to the table.   We both gain: we should not make
the exchange if each did not see his own good in the
bargain.

Plain as this fact is, it has taken a very long time to
make it plain.   What is true of the bootmaker and the
cabinet-maker is true of all the people who live together
and trade together in any one country; it is true of the
trade which is carried on between country and country. It
is no honest man's real interest to make his neighbors poor
and miserable: his best chance is in their wealth and pros-
perity.   But nations have not yet learned this truth. They
still put hindrances between themselves and other nations.

What should we think of a shopkeeper who wished
to sell his own goods, and yet paid a policeman to prevent
the people of another village from coming to buy of him,
and sell to him?   Now this is just what a country does
which prohibits or fetters trade with other countries.

LESSON VI.

THE more employment is divided, the greater is the skill of those who addict themselves to a single employment. "Practice makes perfect," says the proverb. No one can be dexterous without being diligent. By force of habit, persons are able to do things so quickly and so exactly, that they who do not possess the knack wonder how the thing can be done at all. But quickness and exactness mean cheapness, and contribute to what I have called the greatest amount of work with the least possible labor. If everybody had to do every thing for himself, he could not do each thing nearly so well and nearly so easily as would be done if one man made it his business to make one thing, or even part of one thing. It is very useful to know how to do a great many things: it is wise to try to get one's living by making one thing.

Nature points this out to us on a large scale. Different countries have different products. One region grows cotton and tea, another wheat, another rice, another spices, another wine and oil. One country possesses coal, another mines of metals. This division of material qualities points to a division of industries and employments, and an exchange of the benefits which those industries procure.

Similar facts apply to the inhabitants of any one country.   In nearly all parts of the United States, agriculture
is still the prevailing industry; but while in the Northern
and Western States the inhabitants have devoted themselves to the growing of wheat, oats and corn, in the
Southern States the farmers produce principally cotton,
rice, and sugar.   In some parts of the country, moreover,
while a large portion of the territory is still devoted to
farms, a large proportion of the inhabitants are engaged
in other employments, as in New England in manufactur-
ing, and in Pennsylvania and other States in mining and
working metals.   The United States have a long line
of sea-coast, containing many harbors, while the sea in
the neighborhood of some parts of this coast swarms
with fish.   Hence the callings of the sailor and the fish-
erman.

Again, there are occupations which seem to be
proper to sex and age.   It seems natural that men
should do particular kinds of work—as that of a collier,
a glassblower, a smith.   No one would like to see
women engaged in these callings.   Again, some occupations seem peculiarly fitted to women—as that of
teaching children, sewing, and domestic labor.   The
difference of fitness does not lie in the hardness of the
work.   Labor in a harvest field is hard enough, but in
most countries of Europe, in the agricultural districts
women bear a part in this.

Some kinds of work are undertaken by young persons.   It is cruel and foolish to give children hard work.
It is too great a strain on their powers, and therefore
stunts their growth and damages their health.   It interferes with their school-time and learning, and therefore
stunts their minds.   Hence the law in England, and in

some of the United States, prohibits the employment of children below a certain age—at least in certain callings —and does not allow them to work more than a certain number of hours any week during another time of their life. It has been proved, however, that when children of a certain age do light work for a time, and learn for a time, their education does not suffer.

A variety of circumstances, then, lead to a division of employments. Experience shows that such a division makes work easier.

The most familiar and general of such divisions is that which sets a father to work, and gives the mother the management of the home. The wise expenditure of wages is as important and difficult as the skilful earning of wages. No man is more to be pitied than a workman who, having a young family, loses his wife, except perhaps one who has a wife who neglects her duties to her home and her children.

The largest example of the division of employment is to be found in the government of a country. If no arrangement were made for the public and private defence, for doing right between persons in courts of law, but everybody had to undertake the protection of his own home and family from violence, and to be the judge of his own rights and wrongs, the waste of such a system would be vast, the confusion would be constant, and society could not hold together. The soldier, the policeman, the judge, the ruler, are all appointed to the offices they fill, because it is the cheapest course to have such persons to do a great public service.

If you were to go into a great manufactory, you would find in one place a number of persons engaged

2*

in keeping accounts, and considering what work is to be undertaken. Then, when you go into the workshop, you would find a number of persons engaged in various kinds of labor. You might find some men occupied in work which requires a great amount of skill, others in work which needs little more than an effort of strength. You may find women employed in occupations which do not need much heavy labor, but which do require a certain amount of taste or quickness. And, lastly, you may find a number of children occupied in that which does not require much strength or much skill. There may be, in short, many kinds of labor engaged under the same roof.

Now it is plain that there may be, and is, a great variety in the value of these kinds of labor. It would seem that the work which needs much skill and strength ought to be more costly, *i. e.*, be better paid, than that which needs only strength, or only skill, and much more than that which needs neither skill nor strength in any great degree.

Now imagine that one man did all the work. Suppose that he is engaged in something that is really wanted, and which people will freely pay for in order to possess it. It is clear that in such a case he must be paid for the easiest and simplest work at the same rate that he is paid for the hardest and that which needs most skill, and therefore that what he makes and sells will be very expensive.

The division of employment takes away part of the cost of labor. Easy work is paid at cheap or low rates; hard work, and work which needs much skill, at high rates. In a great factory, such as I have spoken of, one workman may earn as many dollars a week as another earns dimes. Nay, the most important workman of all, the manager, has, if he is paid properly, to receive much more than any of those who are put under him, and for a very plain reason.

LESSON VII.

JUST as one field may grow more corn than another field, without putting the farmer to any greater cost in cultivating it,—just as a shop in one street may be more suitable for business than an equally good shop in another street,—just as one mine may yield more coal or iron than another mine, while the cost of working both is the same, and so on with a variety of other such naturally useful objects—so one man may, with no greater cost of preparation than his neighbor, earn a great deal more than that neighbor. There is a superior fertility of certain fields, a greater profit to be got in certain places, richer veins in certain mines, and similarly there is a greater natural power in certain minds. Two lawyers may have the same education and be equally diligent, but one may earn hundreds where another only earns tens. Two physicians may have had the same advantages of study, and have equally striven to profit by their opportunities, and one may make a fortune while the other can barely earn a living.

Now in the case of the field, the shop, and the mine, it is easy to measure the natural advantage which the more favored possess over the less, for reasons which I gave before, when I told you how rent arises. It is not so easy, however, to measure the advantage which superior abilities give some persons over others who work in the same calling; but they are none the less real and solid.

These advantages of superior natural powers are to be noticed more frequently in mental labor than in manual. When an ordinary manual laborer has superior gifts, he seldom remains long in his first calling. He contrives to raise himself to what may be called the professional class, to leave off working with his hands, because he is able to work with his head. The history of invention contains many instances of persons who have begun their career in a very humble station, and who have raised themselves to great eminence by their genius and skill.

I have mentioned this difference of capacity between man and man, because it is the only fact which prevents the rule which I am going to state from being universal —that the wages of every kind of labor or service which is offered and accepted are measured by the cost of producing and maintaining the laborer. As the mass of men have no remarkable gifts, the rule holds in their case without exception.

I use the words "labor or service which is offered and accepted," because when a thing is not wanted it has no price or value. In degree, as I have said before, the same fact prevails when more is offered than is wanted. I put the case where the quantity offered exactly satisfies the quantity needed, because we are able to discover from such a case what follows when the offer is more than the want, or the want is more than the offer.

From time to time every kind of labor rises and falls in value because more or less of it is needed. When in 1862, and for two or three years afterwards, there was a very scanty quantity of cotton to be sold, and therefore the price rose greatly, the services of cotton-spinners in England were less needed, and in consequence great distress prevailed in those English counties where the chief industry is that of cotton-spinning. When, a few years ago, it was no longer found to be worth while to build iron ships on the Thames, the same kind of distress occurred among the ship-builders.

Taking these cases into account then, we shall find that the rule given above holds good. A workman is not paid wages in proportion to the importance of the service he does, or to the general skill with which he does it, but according to the cost of making him fit for the work which he has to do.

There is no workman who can do so many things well as a good farm-laborer. He can plough. Now this is a work which requires a nice eye and a steady hand, for the ploughman has to drive a straight furrow for a long distance, and make that furrow of a uniform depth. He can reap—a task which requires no little skill; mow; build up a rick, thatch it; tend horses sheep, and cattle; milk cows; trim hedges; clean and bank ditches, and a number of other things, any one of which needs great skill: but he is generally paid very low wages.

The fact is, it costs very little to fit him for his work. At an early age he is made to earn the whole or part of his living, by being set to work in the field. He picks up his skill in other kinds of farm-work gradually.

There are other callings in which it is the custom to limit the right of working to those who have been apprentices, and further to limit the number of apprentices which a master may take. These rules make laborers scarce. The first rule makes the cost of training high, by delaying the power of earning full wages; the second rule makes the number of laborers few. In callings therefore where these rules prevail, the wages of the workman—whose skill, maybe, is far less than that of the farm-laborer—are far higher than those of the farm-hand. But I must speak more at length on this subject hereafter.

A workman, in short, is just like a machine. It costs a great deal to render him competent to do work, and the outlay varies from hundreds to thousands of dollars. The workman has to be provided with food in order that he may work at all, just as a machine has to get its power of motion from fuel or some other source of power; and similarly, the human machine lasts in its full strength only for a time, and entirely wears out at last.

If there were any plan devised by which all the workmen in a particular calling were brought up and taught at the public expense, the wages of such workmen would reach the lowest range. In so far as some of such workmen were thus bred up, so far the wages of all would be lowered. There is no doubt, since many children of the poorest classes are brought up at the public expense in workhouses and elsewhere, that the general rate of wages is thereby lessened. There are some gifts which are not gains; you may not be able to refuse their acceptance, though you may be none the better for them.

LESSON VIII.

UNPAID WORK.

THE hardest labor which men undergo in field factory, or mine, is not so hard as that which some undergo
merely to amuse themselves. There are men who hunt,
swim, race, row, run, walk, in a manner which, if they
were forced to do these things by another's will, or for
their living, would be a grievous hardship—a mere cruel-
ty. So there are people who study. A man will gaze
night after night at the stars with a patience and earnest-
ness which few give to their common business—with far
more diligence than any switch-tender watches trains.
Another will pore over coins, and relics, and ruins, for
months and years together; and not only will such people work very hard, but they will get nothing for their
trouble.

This kind of work is generally very pleasant to the
man that undertakes it, and is sometimes very useful to
society. Unless it goes into excess, exercise is of great
service to the man who takes it. It makes him healthy,
clear-headed, and strong; it gives, or ought to give, a
lesson of temperance, for no person can excel in those
exercises unless his habits are regular and sober. The
change also from one kind of exertion to another is exceedingly good for boys and men. A boy who mopes

in the playground seldom makes much figure in his class.

These exercises are a good thing for society at large. It is everybody's interest that the men and women of the nation to which he belongs should be healthy and vigorous. A plant is healthy by reason of its leaves as well as its root; a man is healthy when his mind and his body grow together. Now a race of stunted, sickly people may be said to be like a growth of stunted and sickly plants. Happily, however, it is almost always possible to put health into young people. It has sometimes happened, though, that a race has been ruined.

Again, when an astronomer watches the skies night after night—a geologist studies the manner in which the earth is constructed—a naturalist busies himself with the different habits and powers of animals—a botanist inquires into the structure of plants—these people are engaged in occupations which give them the keenest pleasure. The study of nature is one of the best and most gratifying of pursuits. You can follow it out in a great town as eagerly, though not perhaps as fully, as in a country village. It will give a relish to all occupations, and add new powers to one's eyes, and sometimes to one's other senses.

These pursuits give a great many advantages to him who follows them. It would be sufficient if they afforded him a rational amusement, and lifted him above merely sensual pleasures; but they very often do much more. Observing eyes have frequently found out something which have set many heads and hands to work. The prizes of human life are rare, and many may miss them who deserve them as much as those who find them, but nobody ever found them who kept his eyes shut.

But I am more concerned at present with the effect of these kinds of study on society at large. They have constantly been the reason why mankind has made a great and lasting advance from weakness to power; and there is no doubt that they will constantly produce the same results. It is easy to prove what I have said.

Some student finds out that a little piece of stone gives a power to a little piece of steel of always pointing in one direction. His discovery enables sailors to improve the art of navigation, and to find out a new world.

Still, this discovery only tells the sailor which way he is going. Another person finds out that he can make, by reason of the qualities of certain metals, an instrument which will measure time with almost complete accuracy, and thus enable the sailor to find out where he is.

The ship is, however, a very rough affair. Another person studies the properties of water, air, and wood, and defines, as accurately as a reckoning in figures will define any thing, what are the rules by which a ship should be built.

Now let us take another subject. A student busies himself with the ground on which he walks, the quarries of stone which are dug out in it, and the shells and other relics which he finds in it. He is struck with the fact that the shells are exactly the same as those which are found near such coal-mines as are or have been worked. He argues, and he is right too, that though no coal is to be seen in the place which he has examined, the coal will be found on digging. He does the same with mines of metals.

A chemist is engaged in trying, for the pure love of

knowledge, to find out what are the properties possessed by gas-tar. Nothing, it would seem, but a love of science would lead him to trouble himself with it. But he knows that Nature is full of pleasant surprises, and that the more you learn about it, the more you enjoy it. By-and-by he finds out that this black, ill-smelling stuff contains the material for the most brilliant colors which can be given to cotton, wool, and silk.

Hardest of all, a man busies himself with considering how the life of man can be spent most profitably to his neighbor and himself—how the world can go on with the least possible waste and disappointment. If he hits on the truth, he has done the rarest work of all, chiefly because the fruit of his discovery is to teach the way in which each man can make the best use of his powers. His work is of a very anxious kind, partly because it is so serious a matter if he makes a mistake, and persuades people that his mistake is a truth, partly because it is so difficult to discover the truth after which he is seeking.

Perhaps not one of these persons is ever paid for his trouble. Many of them do not care to be paid, and if their work were ever so much slighted, would persevere as steadily as though it were reckoned at its true value.

I have spoken of these cases because it must not be supposed that all useful work is paid for. Had it not been for such persons as these, who have studied what is to be seen and known for truth's sake, there would have been very little real progress made by mankind. Social science takes note of those services especially which are valued and exchanged; but it would be a great mistake to forget that some of the best services are beyond value, and cannot be priced, because no known price equals their worth.

LESSON IX.

MOTIVES FOR LABOR.

IT does not follow because a man works for that which will give him wages or profit, that he does not feel a pleasure in his work. Men may have a keen eye for the advantages which their calling affords them, and yet have as keen a love for the calling itself. A great painter, like Turner, may be quite devoted to his art, and yet be quite alive to the gain he makes by it. A great musician may be excessively fond of the wonderful subject on which his genius is exercised, as Beethoven was, and yet drive a good bargain with those who prize his compositions. It is a great mistake to think that the toil by which a man earns his bread must needs be unpleasant. On the contrary, he is a very silly fellow who does not make it agreeable, if it be possible to do so. But there is no doubt that every man who works for his living wishes to shorten his labor as much as he can. So also does he who works for his pleasure. Provided it be only well done, no sensible person likes to linger over his work longer than he can help.

Now, what is it that sets most men and women to work? It is necessity. A man must work in order to live. A few people can live without working in any society, but only a few. Nay, it is remarkable that of these few a great many work very hard, some for profit, some for glory, some for what they believe to be the good of their fellow-men. In our country there are many rich but very few idle persons. Some of the richest are the most active, and if you remember what was said in the last lesson, some of them are the most useful.

A man, however, may be very willing to work, and yet find nothing to do, because he has not found anybody who wants that which his work produces. Makers of carpets and fire-irons would find no employment in Brazil, for in a hot climate nobody uses a carpet or keeps a fire in his sitting-room.

Somebody wants a man's work before he betakes himself to such an industry as he carries on. Somebody is ready to pay for it—that is, to give money for it, or to exchange something else for it—that is, to make something which he will give instead of it. For reasons which I shall show in another lesson, to buy and to barter are really the same things.

Two or more people work, then, because somebody wants what they work at. There are, of course, many kinds of wants, which are more or less pressing. Everybody wants food, clothing, and shelter. But there are many other wants when these are satisfied, which many or few people desire. If they do desire them, and they can be supplied, they get them satisfied.

You will see, then, that the force which sets people to work is twofold: their own needs and the needs of others. If men wanted nothing, they would not work; and if other men would give nothing which they want, it would be no good for them to work.

Now if any man who works could easily and instant-

lỷ find a customer or customers who would keep him in
constant employment, and would give him in exchange
for his work what he wants himself, the circle would be
complete.   Such a state of things occurs to a greater or
less extent in country villages.   A tailor or shoemaker
constantly gets work from the villagers who live in the
same place with him, finding his customers without any
difficulty, and living entirely on their wants. In India the
system is carried out much more exactly.   In the villages of that country there are always a certain number
of artificers who live out of the common funds of the
village, in return for the labors they give.

Remembering, then, that the sole force which moves
a man, whose needs compel him to work, is the willingness of others to buy the proceeds of his work from
him, you will see that our social life, especially with
those who dwell in large towns, is very different from
that which belongs to our country villages, and still further removed from that which is found in India.   The
city workman seldom deals directly with the man who
uses that which he makes; he is generally employed by
a person who is called master.

This master or employer is really a middleman or
go-between.   His business is to find out customers for
the workman's labor, and so to save him the trouble of
seeking the customers himself.   Now such an agent is a
great saving to the workman.   Though he does not say
so in so many words, he does say in effect, "I will find
you persons who will buy your labor, if there are any
persons who will buy it."

Next, his experience in finding customers not only
stands the workman in good stead, but the same experience enables him to guess with fair certainty what the

number of such customers will be, and to take the risk of finding them out. Hence he is able to fix in a rough way how much of the labor for which he finds customers is wanted, and in a much closer way, is able to find regular work for as many laborers as are needed for this work.

There is nothing which a workman desires more than steady work at a fair price. This is what the middleman or employer does for him, or at least offers to do for him. He buys his labor and sells it again. The laborer sells him his labor as really as the merchant sells the employer the leather, wood, cotton, or cloth on which the workman tries his skill. Nay, the workman actually lends his labor, unless he is paid from hour to hour, or the employer advances his wages, as certainly as the man lends money who makes an advance to the employer, in order to enable him to buy the materials which I named just now.

Why, then, is this employer or master paid, and what is he paid? He is paid because he does a service to the laborer, and for the matter of that, to the man who buys the laborer's work in the end. He is paid because he works; and he is paid well whenever his skill is no common power. The employer will and can no more work for nothing than any other laborer can or will. How much he will be paid depends on several things. It depends partly on the bargain which he can make with the laborer, partly on the bargain which he can make with the customer, partly on the shrewdness and skill with which he can guess at what the customers want.

He does not, however, except in a very narrow sense, set labor in motion. He does not find wages, ex-

cept for a short time.   He is a middleman, or go-between, or dealer, who does a very useful service to certain persons, a service which very often is quite necessary.   But many laborers do without him, many more
could do without him; some are doing without him on
a very great scale.   But social life can never wholly get
rid of him, for he is sometimes a real necessity for laborer and customer.

LESSON X.

THE reasons which give a price to the master's or employer's labor, enable the shopkeeper to get a profit on what he does. The shopkeeper is the last link between the laborer or producer, and the customer or consumer. If he were got rid of, or not in existence, the man who makes any useful article would have to hunt out the man who wants the article. This would be a waste of time, and therefore it is better to employ a go-between.

The reason why there are such persons as merchants, agents, bankers, contractors, and so forth, is just the same. These are middlemen, who cheapen, or, what is the same thing, render more convenient the course of trade. Of course, if there are more of them than are needed, they are a hindrance and a loss. When there are too many of them they cause dearness, for they generally unite together to fix the price of what they sell, and then look out for customers. They have a perfect right to do this, for everybody has a right to put his own price on his own goods and his own labor, and if need be, to unite with other persons for a common end; but then, other people have a right to do without them if they choose to do so.

8

No one, it is clear, has a right to demand of any other person that he should find him employment. A man who wants something may make it himself if he pleases, and if he can. A man who needs a service may do it for himself, if he is able, and nobody is wronged. So if a body of workmen or a body of customers can get rid of these middlemen, they are perfectly justified in doing so.

This is sometimes done under what is called *co-operation*. The word is rather an unlucky one, because there can be no human society at all without co-operation; but the word is commonly used to express a particular kind of partnership, in which the service of the middleman is got rid of. Of this partnership there are two kinds.

One, the easiest and the simplest, is that which seeks to get rid of the shopkeeper, and therefore to sell the articles either at the ordinary price, and divide the profits among the customers of the shop or store, or at the lowest cost possible, after the expenses of the shop are paid. Such a scheme has been adopted in some settlements in the United States and in many towns through the North of England. The principle of the plan is that the shop gives no credit, and therefore runs no risk.

The other kind of partnership is where the workmen find building, machines, tools, and materials themselves, and so get rid of the master or employer. This is a much more serious business. If it succeeds, the workmen, in addition to their own wages, get the employer's wages also.

In order that such a plan should succeed, three things are necessary: good management, prompt obedience to the necessary discipline of the workshop, and thrift. It is not difficult to secure the thrift, for when all the workmen, or a vast number of the workmen, are also owners, there is every wish to avoid waste. In this particular, an association or partnership of workmen has a great advantage over an employer. I am told that where this plan has been adopted the saving of waste is often very great. I am afraid it is true, and will be true for a long time to come, that people take more care of their own than they do of their neighbor's property.

It is not always easy, however, to secure prompt obedience. Men who possess their own property don't like to be dictated to sometimes as to how they should use it, and English-American people, we are told, least of all. They make a great mistake when they show this self-will, even though no person's interest but their own is concerned. For, unluckily, the notion that a man will always save and spare what belongs to him, is a great error. Passion, and the habit of thinking only of the present day, instead of the future, make many men waste their substance, their powers, and their character.

But when another man's interest is bound up in one's own, the folly of negligence to duty, or order, or needful obedience, becomes a crime. You may see this best in an army. The safety of all lies in the obedience of all. If there be such a thing as natural rights, to go to sleep when you are tired is one of those rights; but if a sentinel does so, he is shot. Another natural right is that of avoiding danger; but a man who runs away in a battle is treated with the same justice as is given to a sleeping sentinel. It is quite fair that a man should

choose those with whom he cares to have friendship
but in war the choice is restricted, under the same penalties.

Such, or something like it, is the case with a business
in which many persons are interested. If one man neglects his work, another refuses to obey orders, a third
undertakes that which does not belong to him, every
thing is thrown out of gear. You can see the same
thing in a school. The first rule of a school is order.
Out of school the more liberty without wrong-doing
the better: in school hours no liberty and full obedience
is the way to work well. In some of these workmen
partnerships of which I know, obedience is as strictly
maintained as it is in an army; in consequence, the whole
of the workmen prosper.

The hardest of all the needs is good management;
but the better and wiser the workman is, the easier is the
management. If there were no wilful, foolish, and
vicious people in the world, there would be no great
trouble in ruling men. If there were no naughty and
idle boys, the government of a school would be very
easy. Perhaps, too, it is not so difficult to find people
who will trust the ruler, as it is to find rulers who can be
trusted.

Now these partnerships of workmen have been entered upon in England and in the United States. They
have been very successful where the plan has been carried out as I have described it; but they have been still
more successful in Northern Germany.

LESSON XI.

THE RIGHT OF A SELLER TO FIX A PRICE.

IN my last lesson I said that everybody has a right to fix the price at which he will sell that which he possesses. This statement is a general rule, to which there may be exceptions.

For example, if a town was besieged, or in other way reduced to great straits, and a few men possessed all the food in the town, it is clear that, reasonable compensation being made, such persons may be constrained to bring the food they have into a common stock. And the ground of such an interference with trade is, that the siege being endured for the common safety of all, or the calamity, whatever it may be, affecting all, the full rights of property must be suspended for a time.

In the same way, if it were necessary suddenly to undertake some work of public defence—as building forts against an enemy, or joining together to put down a riot, or laboring to check an inundation—it would never do to submit to the highest terms which those who might do the work could extort, but all might be justly called on to aid in what would be a common duty and a common interest.

Again, it must be supposed that the person who fixes his price for his work or labor should be free to choose

The law properly interferes to protect the weak against the strong. Hence it is held that the labor of children should be regulated by law; that certain callings should not be followed by women; and sometimes that the hours of labor in the case of young persons should be put under some limit.

But, with such exceptions as these, the general principle is that everybody has a right to fix what price he pleases for that which he has to sell, whether it be labor or goods. In the case of goods, very few people doubt that this right should be fully given; in the case of labor, people are not so much of one mind, though they are much more agreed than they once were.

If a man has the right of fixing the price of his own labor, he has a right to join with others in order to fix the price of all the labor which they may all be willing to sell. If ten, twenty, or two hundred persons can join in a trade partnership (and in some such partnerships the number is reckoned by thousands—as, for example, in a railway), any number of persons can as rightly engage in a labor partnership, and thereupon agree together as to the terms on which they will sell their labor.

And on the other hand, persons who buy labor, or the produce of labor, have an equal right to decide with whom they will deal. If the workman has a choice as to the rate at which he will work, the customer has a choice as to whether he will accept the workman's terms. In the long run, the interests of the two parties to a bargain are so clearly understood that these things right themselves.

When the workmen join together to fix the price at which they will work, the partnership is called a trades-union. I have called it a partnership, for it is just as much such an agreement as is the union of a number of persons to start a bank or make a railway, or work a mine. To refuse this right of partnership to workmen, and to give it to those who sell goods, is to do an injustice.

There is a very plain reason why workmen unite together in such a partnership. The employer of labor, as I said in my last lesson, finds out the market price for that which he buys from the men whom he employs. Now he wants, of course, to get the best price he can, or as I said before, to get the greatest amount of wages for the least possible work. The employer of labor is the manager of a business. Management means work; and work is, as I have shown you, to be paid for. The manager of a business, then, is just as much a workman as the people from whom he buys labor are.

The price which he gets for that which he sells covers the wages which he has paid the workman, the cost of his own materials, which are only labor stored up in useful objects and his own wages. If the price did not cover these items, it is clear that he would be working at a loss, and would not therefore continue his work. In one shape or the other, then, he gets wages for the work he does.

Now it is possible to conceive that the workmen whose labor he buys may say to themselves, and then to each other: "This employer of ours gets too much wages for his work, and we get too little. We must try to put this right, and see whether we cannot get a larger share. How shall we set about this?"

There are three ways of arriving at such a result. One is, that the laborers should cease to work until they are paid more of the price at which the article which they make sells. Then they are said to *strike*—*i. e.*, to leave off working till their claims are met. Unluckily for the workmen, they are not generally so well informed as the master or employer is as to the price which their labor will fetch, and as to the needs of those who buy from their employer. Hence it has very often happened that when they strike for higher wages they waste their own means, and do not gain the end they strive for. They are as much justified in trying to better the price of their labor, as a tradesman or merchant is who says he will rather not sell at all, than not get what he thinks his goods are worth.

Another way of meeting the difficulty is to submit the whole case to some umpire. People seldom judge of their own rights wisely, and are frequently the better for taking counsel about them. You see this in the games which you play, and when you get older you will see the same fact in a hundred different things. There is a proverb, that "a man who is his own lawyer has a fool for his client." But a man who makes himself the judge of his own rights is even more certain to commit errors. Since this appeal to an umpire began to be practiced in disputes between workmen and employers, a great many difficulties have been settled in a friendly manner.

There is yet a third course; this is to get rid of the employer altogether, and to enter into a complete partnership, in which the manager of the business has the ordering of the labor, and in which the wages of the employer, after paying the manager, are divided among those who work with their hands. But this, as you will see, is what I spoke about in my last lesson, when I told you of labor partnerships. It is not perhaps possible to make this change in all cases, but where the plan has been tried it has often succeeded, and as time goes on it is likely to succeed more and more. Meanwhile the trial points out to workingmen what is the real position in which the employer stands to them.

3*

LESSON XII.

OF course, if workmen had the means wherewith to build the factories in which they work, and to buy the machines, if any, which shorten their labor, the materials on which to work, and could also bide their time till they can sell that which they make to the best advantage, they would be doing what the employer does for them when he uses his property for these ends. If, moreover, having these advantages in their possession, they could find a proper and fit person to direct their work, were content to follow orders, and to use thrift, their own interests would lead them to enter into the partnership, and so save themselves the cost of using the employer's property and services.

They are seldom able to do so. Workmen are rarely worth more than their week's wages in advance, and sometimes not even so much, but have to run in debt until they are paid their week's wages at the end of the week's work. Even if they have saved something, they seldom know how to set about creating such a partnership as I have referred to. They do not see how to begin.

Besides, in a great many kinds of industry a very great outlay has to be made before any returns come in

For example, a railway may be many years in making, before those who have made it can get a profit or reward for their expense. In other words, the property is sunk in the undertaking.

Of course, it is possible for workingmen to find this outlay if they could join together to do so. The sum of money which has been put into the savings banks in this country is far in excess of the capital of the biggest railway. There are now working, and at a very good profit, two cotton mills at Oldham, in England, the largest capital of which has been subscribed in small sums by workingmen.

In by far the largest number of cases, however, some one, two, or more persons called employers, capitalists, or masters, find all the property necessary to make the workshop, buy the machines and materials, and hold the goods. This is what they do. They do not really pay the workman, for at the end of the week they are in debt to him for work he has trusted them with. They merely buy his labor, as much as they buy whatever else they want; and they sell what they have bought to the customer.

Now you will see that the property with which the employer gets together buildings, machines, materials, and on which he can live till he sees proper to sell what he has bought, is only so much labor previously spent. We saw before that, with one exception, nothing has any value except by reason of the work which has been laid out on it. Property is value put into material objects by means of labor.

Some motive, however, must be put before the person who owns this property in order to induce him, instead of using it for his own enjoyment or amusement,

to save it first, and then to employ it in assisting others
to work. It is true that the owner of such property
would not use it in this manner, unless he expected
to get it back again in its full value; and get something else as a reward, so to speak, for employing it
to the good of others, instead of devoting it to his own
pleasure.

This reward or inducement is called *interest*. A man
lends, so to speak, seed to the ground, and he expects
not only to get back his seed at harvest-time, but a great
deal more than he lent. In the same way, if a man puts
property into the ground—for example, builds a house,
drains a marsh, buys cattle and sheep to fatten, he ex
pects to get his cost price back again, sooner or later,
and something more. In just the same way if he lends
property to another, he expects to get repaid with some
thing into the bargain.

There is no doubt that the services of what is called
capital, and for the use of which interest is paid, are
very important; but we must take care against two mis-
takes. We must not use the word in too narrow a
sense; we must not overrate the importance of that
sense in which the word is commonly used.

In the first place, as I have told you before several
times, there is no value in any thing which does not cost
labor. Now any thing on which labor has been bestowed,
and which people are desirous of using or buying, is capital. A grown workman whose work is worth any thing
at all, is as much capital as a machine, or a useful animal, or any other kind of property whatever. If a
thousand workmen are employed by a builder, each one
of these men brings capital into the business as much as
the employer does who brings bricks, stone, lime, timber

ladders, and the like. All useful things which can be sold are wealth, and all wealth that can be used is capital. In the wages which are paid to workmen for their work, part is interest on the charge laid out in making the workman fit for his calling; part is the cost of finding him food and other necessaries; part is what is required in order to bring up other workmen (his children), to fill his place when he is gone; part is, or ought to be, a fund for him when he is sick or aged, and unable to work.

Next in the common meaning given to " capital "— *i.e.*, the property employed to keep work going on steadily—it must not be supposed that the capital sets the laborer to work. What sets him to work is the needs of those who will use his work. There is a sense in which the steam-engine and the water-wheel set a flour-mill to work. In such a sense the capital of the employer may be said to set labor to work; but every child will see that the real cause which sets such a mill to work is the willingness or wish of people to buy flour. Sometimes people talk as though the workman were under an obligation to his employer, or as if the former depended entirely on the latter. Each depends on the other, just as the blades of a pair of scissors do, before they will cut any thing, and the advantage is mutual.

The employer, therefore, gets wages for the work he does just as the workman does; but he also gets an interest on the property he lays out. So does the workman; but the interest which the workman gets is mixed up with his wages, and in order that it may be found out, such an examination as I have given you is needed.

LESSON XIII.

THE USE OF GOLD AND SILVER.

I HAVE said, several times, that men are led to work by their wants, and that the work which one man does is exchanged against the work which another man does. The agents for bringing about this exchange are those middlemen who are called employers, merchants, or shopkeepers, as the way in which they do this service differs or varies.

But it is very rare to see goods bartered against goods; it is never the case that they are valued against each other. Generally people take bits of metal instead of goods, and they always reckon the value of what they buy in these bits of metal. In common language, they give a *price* to what they sell or buy.

Now why should people do this? Bits of gold, silver, and copper do not seem to have any real use; they do not satisfy any of the great needs of life. The utmost use one can put them to is to fasten them to one's clothes, in order to make one's self look smart. Some people do this. And yet everybody is willing—nay, anxious—to take these pieces of metal.

The fact is these pieces of metal save a vast deal of trouble. If it were not for them, the workman who has made a chair, and wants to buy bread, would have to find a baker who wants a chair, before he could get his wants supplied; and this, I need hardly say, would cause a terrible waste of time. Clearly there is only one thing to do. It is necessary to discover something which everybody is willing to take. If this be once found out, there will be no difficulty in the chairmaker getting bread, provided some one is found who will buy his chair.

Now I have said that everybody is willing to take money, and because everybody is willing to take it, it is the easiest thing to get rid of, the most convenient means with which to supply one's wants. There is nothing which is generally so easy to sell as money—at least under ordinary circumstances. During the late siege of Paris it was not so easy to sell it, because food and similar necessaries were so scarce; but when nothing out of the way happens, there is no object which gives its possessor so much power over property.

The man who takes it does not mean to keep it. It does not increase in value because he keeps it. The only way in which it can be turned to account is to get rid of it. A person who hoards or saves it does not do so merely in order to keep it, for a bag of stones would in such a case, as the old fable says, be as good as a bag of money is, but because he knows he can get rid of it when he pleases with advantage or pleasure to himself. They who save to the most purpose get rid of their money the quickest, either by buying articles to trade with, or materials to work on, or by hiring labor, in the making railroads, building houses, and the like, or in lending it to those who do those things.

The sooner the money, then, passes from hand to hand, the better does it serve the purpose for which it

was discovered and adapted.   It is intended to *circulate*.
It is called currency, from a Latin word which means *to
run ;* because the more speedy is its action, and the
more numerous are the bargains for which it is used,
the more useful do people find it.   For the same reason
those countries which are the busiest, and which therefore use their money to the most purpose, are able to do
with fewer pieces of money than other countries where
the same speed of circulation is not attained.

How useful money is, may be easily reckoned if one
thinks what would be the consequence if all the money
of a country were suddenly to vanish.   Such an event
would cause the greatest confusion and distress.   In
time, no doubt, matters would right themselves, either
by the fresh introduction of more money, or by the discovery of something else which would serve to measure
the value of things, or by some standard or measure
which should express the market worth of whatever is
wanted.   For though there is no race of men, possess
ing the least civilization, which does not measure the
worth of the things which the people produce and exchange, yet some have no use of metals, employing other
articles instead.

Apart from the convenience which money affords
buyers and sellers on a small scale, it has a further service, as a measure or means of calculating value.

Trade on a large scale is always in goods.   Thus,
for example, if this country trades with France, it buys
French goods with American goods, or with goods
which have been bought with American goods.   Unless
it is found convenient to do so, one country does not
pay the other money ; and when it is found convenient,
the money paid is not really money, but metal, since

French money is not current in the United States, nor is American money in France.

But though no money passes between the two countries, the American merchant makes out his bill in dollars and cents; the French merchant his in francs and centimes. These different kinds of money are compared at a certain rate—*i. e.*, five francs and a fraction are reckoned to be worth an American dollar. Nor would it be possible to carry on the trade between the two countries, except on the basis of some such reckoning. There are different qualities of goods—say of wine and cloth—and these qualities must be expressed in some form, standard, or measure.

Children who read this little book, no doubt, have learned a little of what are called vulgar fractions. Now you cannot add fractions, or subtract fractions, without finding out the common denominator, as it is called, of the two quantities which are to be treated. So it is with exchanges. You cannot strike a bargain until you have agreed upon some measure which shall give the worth or the price of these objects which are to be exchanged.

Money then, or a measure of value, is not only a convenience but a necessity; and a strange thing about it is, that it is most necessary, even when it is not actually used.

LESSON XIV.

MONEY.

It is not so very difficult to see why people must take something by which they may measure the value of every thing else, and how inconvenient it would be were no such standard or measure to be found. But why have they chosen bits of two metals to be the means for this measurement? It seems as though it were impossible for any society of men to make any way in civilization, unless they have some such means of bargaining. But why take gold and silver as the general and ready reckoners of all values?

Now my readers may perhaps remember that I have said, more than once, that the value of all objects, services, articles, etc., is measured by the cost of getting them. It will be clear also that in taking something which shall measure any other thing, it is of importance that the measure itself should change as little as possible. Apart from their use as money, gold and silver have other and very important uses, and therefore are liable to vary in value as well as other things do.

But within a limited period—such a time I mean as a person would keep gold and silver by him—these articles change less in value than any other thing besides Over a long period they are subject to changes in value. Thus, a pound weight of silver, five hundred years ago, would have bought four times as much of the necessaries of life as it now would. But from day to day, week to week, year to year, money varies in value less than any thing else. There are two reasons for this. First, gold and silver are generally obtained in nearly equal quantities at nearly equal cost. You hear sometimes of some lucky miner who has found a great lump of gold, or has come across some very rich vein of silver; but these things are rare. The great majority of those who seek for either give a great deal of labor for every ounce or pound they get; so much labor that nothing but the very high price they obtain for these metals would induce them to work for them at all. The labor which gets gold out of rocks is very costly. It exists, as a rule, in such small quantities in very hard rocks, that it cannot be seen, but can be gathered only by crushing the rock to powder, and then mixing it with another metal, which has the property of melting out the gold, in just the same way that water dissolves salt.

There have been times in history when gold and silver have been obtained at greatly diminished cost. This was the case in the sixteenth century, when the Spanish conquerors of the New World became the possessors of great quantities of silver, and by their means the rest of the civilized world procured it. This wealth was obtained by the enforced labor of the native people, and was therefore, as far as the Spaniards were concerned, cheaply won. But such occurrences are very rare, and for the sake of humanity we will hope that they will never recur.

Next, the stocks of the precious metals—as gold and

silver are called—are so large, that any notable increase to their quantity in any one year will have little effect in diminishing the value of that which has already been collected. If the crops in any one year are greatly in excess of those which are generally garnered, the prices of farm-produce will greatly fall, since most of that which is produced in any year is consumed in the same year, or before the next harvest. And on the other hand, when there are very scanty crops, there is a great rise in the price of such produce. But the stock of gold and silver already existing is very large, and therefore a great increase obtained in any one year is lost in the far greater quantity which society possesses. If a storm occurs in the mountains, the little brooks swell speedily into great torrents; but if there be a vast lake into which these torrents fall, very little effect will be produced upon it by the quantity of water which has fallen in any storm, however heavy may be the fall of water during the time the rain lasts.

Next, gold and silver represent great value in small compass. To get them requires great labor. They are generally found in regions where there is little else, whither the food of the miner has to be carried at great expense; and they are obtained by expensive processes. Were these metals cheaply got, their use would be seriously lessened, as it would take so much of each in order to exchange for goods.

Next, they are almost incapable of being destroyed. Gold is not tarnished by any natural substance, silver by hardly any; hence they suffer no waste by being kept and used, beyond wear. A man who takes gold and silver expects that hereafter he will be able to get rid of them, on as good terms as he could have obtained when he received them; but he would not be sure of this if they wasted, or underwent any change.

Again, they may be cut up into small pieces, and put together again with ease. A weight of gold and silver is of the same value whether it be in small or large pieces. In many objects small pieces are of little or no value, while large pieces are of great value. This is the case with precious stones, for the large are scarce, and the small by comparison common. Little and great however, would be of equal value, if the stones could be melted into a mass as easily as pieces of metal can.

Lastly, they are capable of being marked in such a manner as that even a child can understand their value. This marking or coining pieces of money is always the business of Government, because it is of great consequence that the fineness of the money, and also the weight of the piece, should be certified, though the former is the most important. To issue base money is a great offence, not only because it is a particularly mean kind of stealing, but because it is one which puts the greatest hardship on those who can bear it the least—namely, the poor and inexperienced.

The above are the qualities which, being possessed by gold and silver, and being shared by no other objects whatever, have caused those metals to be chosen by almost universal consent, as the measure of value and the means of exchange. When they are supplied, and can be used, they are always accepted by races which are capable of being civilized; while such races as will not or cannot use them always melt away before more robust and vigorous nations, since their ignorance and incapacity puts them to so serious a disadvantage beside their neighbors and rivals.

These metals may be compared to the oil which makes machinery go smoothly. The force of the machine is given it when it is completed and moved; but unless oil is supplied to the joints, valves, or axles, the machine cannot continue in motion, but is speedily clogged and stopped.

LESSON XV.

SUBSTITUTES FOR MONEY.

AMONG the reasons which have induced men to adopt gold and silver as a means for carrying on trade is, as I have said before, that these metals represent great value in small compass. But this very reason induces the people who use them to use as little as they can of them. They cost very much, and therefore men strive to lay out as little cost as possible on them. Now there are two ways in which the use of these metals is narrowed. One is to make each piece do for as many acts of trade as possible, or in other words, to change hands as often as may be.

Unless men trust each other, they are obliged to take every possible care against risk. In a country where there is little confidence between man and man, where trust is warily and scantily given, there is need for far more money than in a country where confidence and mutual trust are the rule. Everybody who is not living from hand to mouth keeps some small stock of money in his possession, in order to meet his every-day wants; but when distrust is general, prudence requires persons to keep a larger stock of this kind of property, and consequently to use more money. The civilization of a country is not measured by the amount of gold and silver which it has, but by the integrity, mutual trust, and intelligence of its inhabitants. It is possible that the people of a half-barbarous country like Turkey may have more money than a thriving and busy country like our own; but the money is not turned to so good an account.

The other way in which the use of money is saved, is to discover some substitute for its use. Now, long ago, persons have found out that bits of paper, having no value in themselves, but giving the possessor of them a right to claim a sum of money, would, in many particulars, serve the purpose of the real money, and in some cases would be more convenient. This substitute for the use of money is called a bank-note.

Now it is not to be expected, in a little work like this, intended for beginners in social science, that I can enter into all the peculiarities belonging to such a use of printed pieces of paper; the subject would be too long, and the explanation in detail would be too difficult. But in order to understand this part of the social system under which we live, it is almost necessary to know a little about the use of these pieces of paper, since they play so important a part in trade and exchange.

It is no use to try to circulate these pieces of paper, unless the person who takes them is quite certain that he will get the sum of money which they profess to be worth, whenever he wishes it. Men take money itself because it is the most convenient and ready way of supplying their wants. A man with five dollars has a much greater command over what he needs, than a man has with five dollars' worth of goods—as of shoes, bread, or furniture.

So if men take any thing which pretends to represent

money, it is no use to offer them something instead of money, however valuable that may be which is offered. If the piece of paper promises to pay them five dollars, it will not satisfy them if the person who pledges to pay this money offers to pay them five dollars' worth of something. If they suspect that the person who promises money intends to pay them something else, they will not take and use his bits of paper, or will not use them very long.

Plain as this may seem to us, it has taken a very long time to make the rule understood. At different times, governments have tried to circulate such pieces of paper, and in place of giving money, have offered land, or other property. The attempt has always been a failure—a loss, and occasionally a great public misfortune.

Now if the pieces of paper thus put out were exactly equal in value to the money for which they are used, and exactly that sum of money were kept by the person who promised to pay the quantity of money which each of these papers represent, no gain or advantage would be made by the persons who circulate the paper; but a certain loss would be incurred in the labor of preparing these pieces of paper, and in that of keeping an account of them. They who use the paper would have some advantages. The gold and silver would not wear at all, and the loss of the piece of paper need—with proper care taken—be no real loss to the person who possessed it, because if he could give an account of the paper, he might, in time, be repaid its value.

But the persons who put this paper into circulation find out, after a time, that they can send a great deal more of these papers out than they have money at any moment to pay with, provided always that people will trust to

4

them. The rest they can employ in other objects, taking care to have their property in such a shape that if there be some sudden need for more money, they shall be able to get it together in a very short time. In other words, the promise to pay will be taken as readily as real money will, and for a time do everything that real money does.

The sending out these bits of printed paper is part of the business which a banker carries on. It is not indeed his only business, for he does other things which are, as I have said, too difficult for beginners in this subject to understand. This, however, I hope they will understand—that a bank-note is something which may be used instead of money; that its use saves some of that very expensive article, and that it therefore enables trade to be carried on with some lessening of cost.

I have now pointed out to you what are the general rules which belong to labor and trade, why it is men labor, and why they exchange with each other the produce of their several kinds of industry. This is, from one point of view, an account of the way in which society grows, and is held together. Men live together in order to do each other benefit, to supply each other's wants; and they are able to do this best when each man betakes himself to that kind of work for which he is fittest, and for which his neighbor has some need. Social life is like a vast machine composed of a great number of parts; each of these parts, however, assists the other parts—is necessary or convenient to the working of the whole.

LESSON XVI.

FREEDOM AND SLAVERY.

IF everybody were wise and just; if no wrong were done by man to man, and no injury inflicted on nation by nation; if every man were sure to get the fruit of his labor, to pass his life without suffering injustice—if, in short, there were no bad and cruel people in the world, the sketch which I have given you of social life might be completed in the pages which you have already studied.

Unfortunately, we are far removed from so pleasant a state of things. It is necessary that persons should be protected in the peaceful exercise of their labor, and in the peaceful enjoyment of that which they have earned by their labor. They who have wealth require to be checked, lest they oppress those who are more or less in their power. Those who are poor sometimes need another kind of check, lest they try to violently seize that which they do not possess, but which they see others possess. In brief, the most civilized nation needs law and government, in order that it may be kept together.

Law professes to declare what are rights and what are wrongs, and proposes to defend rights and correct wrongs—to secure each man in the possession of that which really belongs to him, and to protect him from any attempt on the part of others to interrupt his enjoyment of that which does belong to him. These rights, again, either belong to a man's person or to his property—by property being meant whatever a man has lawfully obtained, and which, within certain limits, he can enjoy.

Now one of the most important rights which a person can be held to possess is that over his own labor. Nearly every civilized nation has agreed that no person can acquire a right to the perpetual labor of another person —or, in other words, make him a slave. At different periods of their history all civilized nations have allowed the right of a master over a slave; now nearly every nation refuses to allow it, and in case any person claims such a right, will decline to enforce it, and will give a remedy against all such as pretend to keep persons in slavery.

Now how comes it to pass that so great a change as this has come over the spirit of civilized life? Slavery prevailed in ancient Greece and Rome—two societies as much civilized in many particulars as we are.

I believe that the first motive which led men to raise the question whether slavery was not always a wrong, which never could be justified, was the feeling that every man has certain natural rights, and that if he has any, personal freedom must surely be the first of these rights, seeing that, if it be absent, no other right can belong to him.

When persons began to hold this opinion, they found out speedily other reasons against holding men in perpetual bondage. It was seen that while slavery degrades the slave, it does nearly as much mischief to the owner of the slave. It is impossible to quench the wish for freedom, at least if any chance of escape appears to the slave; and thus it became, or seemed to become, the interest of the slavemaster to make his slave ignorant and wretched, to reduce him as much as possible to the condition of a beast. Now no one can treat his fellow-man in this way without becoming brutal himself.

Again, it was seen that if a man were to be kept in slavery, the law must put very little control on the acts of his owner. Now men become civilized, not by indulging passion, but by checking it; not by ruling over others, but by ruling over themselves. The custom of slavery was therefore an aid to barbarism, no assistance to civilization. It produced grave moral evils in society, and was a lasting hindrance to good influences.

Again, it was gradually discovered that where slavery prevails very little progress is ever made in the useful arts. The minds of the ancient Greeks and Romans were very much cultivated. These two nations made remarkable progress in what are called the fine arts. Their architecture and sculpture are even now models, for they have hardly been equalled in the one, and by no means equalled in the other. In the same way they were eminent in poetry and oratory, and they made great advances in many kinds of science. But they knew very little of the useful arts. They had hardly invented a single machine which should save labor—had discovered none of those forces which are so familiar to us. In consequence, despite their great culture, the knowledge they possessed, and the perfection to which they carried such civilization as they had, their whole social system crumbled away against the attacks of certain savage tribes.

The fact is, the motive for saving labor by means of mechanical inventions never came home to them. In the ancient world the labor of the hands was held to dishonor a man, to be fit only for slaves. Now the principal cause which has led men to invent labor-saving machines is the impulse which I have stated before—that, namely, of getting the greatest possible recompense for one's labor, with the least possible outlay of labor. While a man is a slave, since all his labor, and all the fruits of his labor, belong to his owner, there can be no motive to save labor—no motive to the slave, for he will get nothing by it; no motive to the owner, for he disdains to lighten the slave's toil. Where slavery lives, invention is dead.

Whenever free labor competes against slave labor, the former is sure to win the day, the latter to be found expensive and uncertain. I do not mean to say that slave labor has not sometimes been profitable to the owner, but that whenever the two exist together the free man will work more cheaply—that is, to greater purpose than the slave. For it will be seen that the owner has to purchase or rear the slave, and therefore has to set down this article of cost. Then no man who works for another ever works with so much heart as when he is working for himself. A free man may be trusted; a slave always wants an overlooker. You can trust a free man to handle machinery or to manage such work as requires care and attention. But the slave has no motive to take care of that which is trusted to him, and hence he can only be put to the simplest kind of work with the commonest possible tools.

Civilized nations, then, have refused to allow any one man a perpetual right to the labor of another, because freedom of labor is a natural right. But a man who commits crime forfeits to a greater or less extent his natural rights, and among them his natural rights of liberty. Hence all communities have their public slaves—*i. e.,* men condemned for a period, more or less prolonged, to compulsory labor on behalf of the State. To protect its subjects, a Government is obliged to restrain criminals. But it is not right that such persons should subsist in idleness; hence it exacts labor from them, and for reasons conceived to be sufficient, reduces them to the slavery which they have merited.

LESSON XVII.

PARENT AND CHILD.

THERE are certain kinds of property—as that of a master over a slave—which civilized law will not recognize. There is another kind of property—as that of a parent over a child—which the law recognizes to a limited extent. There have been countries in which a father had the same rights over a child which some laws have given an owner over a slave. In ancient Rome the right was even larger and more enduring.

A child owes his nurture and education to his parents. He has received from them benefits of the highest kind, which, though the duty of the parents renders them, are not the less grave to the child. But as law cannot allow the constant submission of one man's liberty to another, so it cannot permit the child to be constantly subject to the parents' will. There is a period when a parent's authority is no longer absolute, however much it should always be respected.

During those years when the child is, in the eye of the law, unable to exercise his own discretion in his occupation, the child is in a sense his parents' property. Custom may shorten or lengthen this time, but there always is a period during which no one interferes with the parents' discretion, certain conditions being fulfilled.

But civilized communities will not allow a parent to injure his child's health or to dwarf his mind by setting him to work too early or too long, and in our time, at last, by denying him education. In many countries education is compulsory—that is, the child must be taught under penalties. It is seen that to deny a child teaching, is to deny him a necessary of civilized life, which is inferior to what are called the common needs of life, only because these must be bestowed whatever else is given.

There are laws which forbid the employment of children in certain kinds of work altogether, which only allow a short time every day or week for employment in others, and which compel work and education to go on together, or at stated intervals. It is plain that by early working or overworking a child, a lifelong injury may be inflicted on them.

It is the business of law to protect the weak against the strong. The greater part of the action of law has this object. To take a man's property from him unlawfully, to give him bodily pain, or inflict on him bodily hurt, to injure his character by false statements, is to lay a strong hand on one who is, in some direction or other, weaker than the wrong-doer. If such violence be permitted, the law fails to do its work.

It is clear, then, why law protects children even against their parents. It does not follow that men will always make a right use of that which is their own, even when affection, duty, or interest might prompt them to do so. And as the good of one person may be made subject to the passion or caprice of another, it is necessary for law to protect the weaker person against wrong. It is seldom the case that parents lose their natural affec-

4*

tion for their children, but they do so often enough to
justify the law in interfering.

Besides, there are some instances in which the judgment of the law is better than that of the individual
man; there are some in which it is worse. Generally
a man can tell better than any law can inform him, what
is the calling in which he is most likely to prosper. A
law therefore which should pretend to dictate to any one
which calling or business he should follow, is a mischievous law. There are some countries where the law con-
strains a son to follow his father's business. Now in
such countries very little progress is made.

The judgment of the law is better, however, than
that of a man on most matters of general interest, particularly when the object for which the thing is done is
neither very near nor very plain. For instance, there
are many kinds of work which no man would ever pay
for, because he is unable to see his own advantage in the
purchase, or because he is not able to keep the advantage
of the purchase to himself. Suppose, for example, that
some man of science were able to prove that there is
coal in the Gulf States, at a depth which might be
worked. Everybody who had land in which this coal
might be found would gain a benefit by the discovery,
but no one person could keep the knowledge to himself.
If, therefore, such a discovery could be made, the law
should reward such a person. Very many examples
could be given of such kinds of work or service.

But the case is still stronger in the matter of general
education. The best result of a good education is that
it enables the man who has it, to do what he has to do
in a far shorter time than he could without it, or to do
that which he could not have done at all without it.

For instance, a savage can seldom count more than ten, and can do nothing beyond this very beginning of arithmetic. A child who has been taught a few rules can rapidly do that by which the cleverest savage would be foiled. A man who has learnt to read and write will learn a soldier's drill in half the time that a wholly ignorant recruit will need for the same result. Education, in short, is to know the best way how to do any thing. It is said that the Northern Germans, who are all educated, are the handiest men in the world, because their minds are trained, and are therefore always alert.

It is not, however, wonderful that ignorant people cannot understand the value of education, any more than deaf men can the beauty of a piece of good music. Sometimes, to be sure, parents who are themselves ignorant can see the advantage which learning gives to him who has it, and are therefore, from natural affection, willing or anxious that their children should gain advantages which they themselves do not possess. But there is no little risk that they will not notice this benefit.

Here, then, the law steps in. It takes as it were the survey of the whole landscape. If your eyes wander over a distant view, such as that which you get from a high hill, or a lofty building, you can gain a general idea of the scene which is spread out before you, though you may not be able to see the faces of those who are in the streets below, or tell what the trees are which rise in the distant fields. So it is with the State. It cannot tell what each man should do for his own particular work, but it can direct, and that with certainty, what must be obtained by all, in order that each may do his own work in the best way.

LESSON XVIII.

PUBLIC EDUCATION.

THE law may insist on the education of the people. There are two reasons why it should do so. One of them is that the educated person is of more use to his fellow-men than an untaught person, or as may be said in other words, is less dangerous to others. The other is that the educated person is more useful to himself. Now if it can be shown that the same process makes a man more serviceable to his neighbor, and more prosperous in his own fortunes, it needs very little argument to prove that the process is a very wholesome one.

I have already said that a man who has been taught one thing, learns other things more quickly than a person who is wholly untaught. A man who has learnt to be a carpenter, and requires to be instructed in the art of a smith, will learn to be a smith sooner than he would if he had been taught no other handicraft. A man who has learned French, or Latin, or Greek thoroughly, will master German more easily than one who has never known any other language than his mother-tongue. He who has learnt only one language, says the proverb, has learnt none. A man who has learned to ride, or to swim, will learn to skate more rapidly than one who has never sat a horse, or kept himself afloat in water.

Of course there are some kinds of teaching which make the mind more easily active than others do—that is, which are better instruments of education. They who have given their attention to the discovery of the best instruments of education always propose to themselves to settle what is the best means for making the mind generally active. Experience has proved that if a person has been taught certain things, he will learn every thing more easily than if he had been taught other things. For example, though a person will not readily learn language, because he has been taught to ride, he will learn to ride more easily when he has been taught language.

The kind of learning which makes a man apt to learn other things is that which gives a man the habit of thinking without seeing—which enables him to follow out in his mind something which may be thought of, without the need of seeing any thing which should remind him of it. Thus mathematics are a great aid to education, because they assist this power. In arithmetic we think of numbers without considering the objects which those numbers represent. In a still more marked manner is this the case with higher mathematics—with algebra, geometry, trigonometry. So language, particularly a language which, having been highly cultivated, has been rendered unchangeable because it has ceased to be spoken, is a very powerful means of mental culture. The study of mathematics and of language gives men the power of exact and rapid thought, and enables them to be quick and intelligent.

When a man learns rapidly, he is plainly able to do his fellow-man a service, sooner and more completely, than he does if he is slow. I am, of course, speaking of those services which, being useful, are understood and valued. A boy is taken as an apprentice to learn some skilful trade. The boy who learns the trade in half the time that another takes, is by far the more valuable apprentice of the two. He begins to earn his cost much earlier. The wisest and the most useful men in the world have taken the pains to learn their work thoroughly, and to do their work well. Now such persons have always been taught some things which have aided them in gaining the special knowledge which they want. In short, there are some kinds of knowledge which are uniformly useful for every other kind of knowledge, and to understand and impart this knowledge is to educate people; to get the knowledge is to be educated, in greater or less degree according as this master knowledge is imparted.

It is still a question as to which is the best kind of master knowledge. It is likely that the question would never have been asked, if there had not been several kinds of training; every one of which is very useful for the end which all education has in view. It is probable that no one will ever be able to answer the question, because there are several kinds of this master knowledge, and so many varieties of mind that one kind of knowledge suits this mind best, another that. The real question is, whether the mind of each person is really trained by what he has learned. Some people grow strong on a meat diet; some on a bread or vegetable diet. The most important thing to those who wish to be strong is, not what kind of food is most suitable generally, but what suits each the best.

Next, education is—as indeed, you will have guessed from what I have already said—a great service to the man who has it. If you have ever noticed a clumsy person trying to do a thing which wholly puzzles him, and a handy person doing the same thing with great ease, you will see how it is a service. You may have seen a person who is unable to do something, and have watched him while he is being taught the way to do it by some one who is experienced. Then as you see the person who is taught brighten up when he learns the way, you will understand how useful knowledge is.

Of course, if a few persons know how to do a thing well, they will have a great advantage over their neighbors. That which to others is a toil, is to them a pleasure. See how painful is the effort by which a boy who is beginning to learn reading, cons over his task, and spells the words. Now look at the same boy when he has got a mastery over that which he has been engaged on, and compare his looks as he reads a pleasant book, with the same looks, if you can remember them, when he began to read. In this way you can understand the advantage which a really able man, who has thoroughly cultivated his mind, has over those who do not possess his gifts.

But suppose everybody were well taught, would any one have an advantage then? It is hard to conceive everybody equally well taught, and therefore a uniform level in all minds. Such a thing will never happen if we can judge of the future by the past; but it is easy to imagine the case of a whole nation which is well educated; there are such nations.

Now such a nation will be vastly better off than other nations which are not so benefited. But it might, indeed, it would be the case, that the education not giving them a special advantage at home, not one of them

would have any advantage over his fellow-countrymen.
Is their education, then, of no value? It is of the greatest. It has made them handy; it has made them work
easier. If they have used what they possess wisely,
they can do the same things with half the toil and labor
that they must have given before they were trained. A
skilled person goes straight to the mark, while an un-
skilled one wastes time in finding out what the mark is,
and what is the way to it.

LESSON XIX.

S ECIAL LEARNING.

THERE is a certain kind of education which everybody ought to have; but it is not very easy to decide
what its extent should be. We know where it begins,
but we cannot say where it should end. All allow that
everybody should be taught to read, to write, and to
reckon; and that he should do these things easily. The
fact is, these three kinds of learning must be got before
any other kind of learning can be. After they are obtained, they are used for getting further knowledge; but
where or when this knowledge should stop is not easy to
say. In a sense, whenever these three needful portions
of knowledge are possessed, people who use their powers never cease learning.

On the other hand, it is certain that there are many
kinds of knowledge, all of which no man can get, for
the reason that no man's life is long enough to collect
them. The most learned man in the world knows only
a portion—probably a very small portion—of that which
can be known. Besides, the rule which I laid down
before, that the greatest results are obtained by a division of employments, holds good in learning as it does
in manual industry. The sum of human knowledge is
so vast, that to know any one branch of it properly re-

quires constant attention. Thus one man learns law, another physic; one man studies chemistry, another mechanics, another geology, and so on. As the gathered knowledge of mankind gets to be greater, the study of all kinds of knowledge is more and more divided or distributed.

Now, when that which people know is saleable, there is no need that anybody should interfere in order that this knowledge should be acquired. This is plainly the case in what may be called the common callings of life. There is no need that people should be instructed in different kinds of industry at the public expense; if they were, they who obtain this knowledge would in the end be none the better for being taught, since as I have already shown, the wages of every calling stand in close proportion to the cost at which the laborer has been prepared for his calling.

There are, however, as I have shown, certain kinds of knowledge which are very valuable, but which are not very saleable. The most serviceable man whom any society can possess is a really great statesman—*i.e.*, a man who can deal wisely and justly with all interests, and can take care that no force or power in society is able to oppress or wrong any other, or take that to itself to which it is not entitled. If the service which such a man does could be reckoned at its true worth, there is hardly any price which is too high for so useful and so rare a service. But nobody ever thinks of paying a real statesman for his services; perhaps because it is so very rare that they do occur, are given, and are accepted. Generally a statesman is paid in honor, though sometimes he does not get that before it is too late.

Other persons, too, engage themselves in pursuits

which are of very great use to mankind; but they often do not find their services saleable, either because nobody sees their usefulness, or because everybody sees the usefulness, and everybody is able, after being shown the way, to do what these people have found out. It is very often the case that something which it is very hard to find out at first, is very easy to copy afterwards. A man may give the labor of half a life to that which another may imitate in five minutes. The very greatest discoveries are often so very simple that people often wonder why they were not found out long before. Some man by his patience and shrewdness has put them so completely into the hands of others, that they can never be forgotten. Take, for example, the arts of printing and of paper-making, and the invention of steam-power.

Now there are several ways in which these persons may be paid. The State—that is, the whole people of any country, acting through its Government—may give a reward to the inventor for the benefit he has conferred on mankind. Thus a sum of money was given to Jenner, the physician who discovered vaccination. This person found out by patient and diligent inquiry that there was a simple and safe means of preventing a hideous and dangerous disease. It is said that small-pox is a disorder which man originally caught from an animal—namely, the camel; and it was found that when the same disease occurred in another animal, the cow, they who caught it from the cow had a very mild or slight complaint, and were afterwards safe.

After Jenner found this out, had proved the truth of his discovery, and told it to others, there was nothing to prevent anybody from using the remedy. Honest

physicians never have secrets, always looking on those
who pretend to medical secrets as impostors, or as they
call them, quacks. They are, most probably, in the
right, when they hold this opinion. So of course Jenner published his discovery. In order to reward him
for his services, in some degree at least, the English nation through its Parliament voted him a sum of money.
I imagine that if he could have kept it a secret, he might
have made a large fortune, such as is made by many who
discover something, make it a mystery, and are praised
afterwards by their admirers, because they have grown
rich.

Let us take another example. Thirty years ago, or
rather more, a person who was employed in the English
Post Office thought out a new notion about the carriage
and delivery of letters. He argued that the carriage
of a letter was a small business, and that all the work
lay in the delivery of it. Hence he suggested that there
should be a uniform rate of charge for delivering letters,
because, the old rule that letters should be charged according to distance, was founded on a mistake. Nothing can be more simple and more clear. It is so plain
a principle that one wonders why it was not seen and
allowed long before Rowland Hill found it out. What
the benefit was to the people, is matter of knowledge to
those who are old enough-to remember the old system,
and how they who were separated from their friends
had to pay a penalty for the right of sending a letter to
them.

Now in this case Hill could not keep his discovery a
profitable secret, since by a kind of chance wisdom,
letters in this and in all civilized countries besides,
are carried by the Government. So he made his plan

known. It was not received with great favor, and for
some time after it had been received and acted on, Hill
was made to feel that it is not always well to be wiser
than other people.   At last, however, it was allowed
that the plan was really a good one.   There was only
one way in which the inventor could be rewarded, and
this was by a gift of public money.   It is very seldom that
public money has been so well bestowed.

LESSON XX.

I HAVE told you of one way in which a great public service, when it cannot be otherwise paid for, is sometimes rewarded. There is another and a far commoner way. The ingenuity of man has been directed into the finding out the art of making all sorts of things property—that is, of putting a limit on the use which may be made of such things. Sometimes this artificial limitation has taken the form of compelling the public at large to buy nothing except what has been made in the country, or at least of putting an extra price in the shape of a tax on that which has been produced in other countries. In the history of this country, a man or a company of men has sometimes conquered a territory, and has been permitted in return to have the sole right of selling certain articles in or from that country. Sometimes none but those who have gone through a certain course of education, and have been duly certified as knowing a particular art or craft, are allowed to practise the art. Sometimes persons have this privilege because they have been for a certain number of times in a dining-room. Sometimes the person who has written a book, or invented some useful thing, is permitted, on condition of his publishing the book, or giving an exact description of what he has invented, and how he makes it, to have the sole right of selling book or invention for a fixed number of years.

There is a defence given for these privileges. It is said—and perhaps in past times it might have been said with truth—that unless persons had this protection or assistance for special industry or intelligence, the world would never have made any progress whatever in art or science. Be this true or not, it is certain that whenever any check is put on any man, so that he cannot exercise his own judgment or choice in what he wants to make, to sell, or to buy, reason should be shown why the restraint is good for the people at large.

In this lesson I shall speak of the last two kinds of property created by law. There are the right which an author has to print his own books, and the right which an inventor has to the profit of his own inventions. Both these rights are secured by law—could not indeed be secured in any other way; for it is plain that when an author prints a book, there is nothing in nature to prevent another person from printing it anew; or when a machinist sells a machine, or other invention, from another person copying what he has made. Now it is manifest that in either case the second person, supposing that he is able to sell the book or the machine as easily and as readily as the author and inventor can, would be using the labor of either to his own advantage, and at no cost to himself. This seems like robbery, for robbery is getting property for which a man has never worked, and to which he has no right.

If it can be shown that the right to exercise one's own judgment in the choice of one's own industry may lead a man into taking another person's work without paying for it, and therefore may seriously hinder very valuable labor, the case in favor of giving an author or an inventor a legal property in his book, or in his invention, is quite made out. There are, indeed, some persons who argue that an author is very considerably protected by the fact of his being the first to sell the work he writes, and that he would be perfectly protected if nobody were able to reprint his book with his name. So it is said, on the other hand, that no invention is ever the produce of one man's mind, but of several, and that the legal right of sole sale only confers on one person a property which is just as much the right of several other persons.

There is a difference between a book and an invention. The author of a book uses a material which is common to any man—namely, the words of a particular language, and sometimes facts which are every one's right; as, for example, when he compiles a history. But the rest of the labor is wholly his own. He chooses the words he uses, and he originates, or supplies from his own mind, the arguments or comments which he constructs or makes. Sometimes he has only taken the language, as when he is a poet. Now it will be clear that no two persons could by any probability have thought of using the same words in the same way. If, for example, a man were to publish a drama word for word the same as one of Shakspeare's, and say that he never read Shakspeare's works, but that by some strange chance he had thought exactly and written exactly as Shakspeare did, we should know what to think of him. Nay, if there were sentences in the drama resembling those of Shakspeare, we should not believe him if he asserted ever so strongly that they were his own com position.

But it is quite possible for two persons, or more than two, to have made at the same time the same invention. There are those who say that there never has been any great discovery made in art or science, except by more than one person; that the difference between a book and an invention is total on this point. It is also said that while it is very easy to reprint a book, it is not so easy to copy a machine, and that therefore there is more need of protection in the former than in the latter.

However this may be, the law creates a right of property in books and inventions, calling the one copyright, the other patent-right. The first of these belongs to the book directly it is published, and after the fulfilment of certain conditions. The latter belongs to an invention only after a legal form is gone through, which is attended with no little expense. In general, the duration of the property in an invention is much shorter than that in a book; and it may be added the right which the law creates is generally more valuable in the former than in the latter case.

The law also creates a property in a name or a symbol. If, for example, an author or a publisher starts a magazine or newspaper under a certain name, the law will not allow another person to take that name. In the same way the law will not permit the imitation of a trade mark. Now the reason for this is twofold. In part, the adoption of a name or symbol which another person has made his own, and which he will of course take care to make distinctive or peculiar, is an invasion of that which may be called his property. In part, it is a fraud which nearly resembles forgery—that is, the imi-

5

tation of a person's signature on an order to pay money
The offence is not so serious, because a successful forgery is a total fraud, against which no pains would secure any one; while an imitation of a trade mark merely substitutes one man's goods for another's.

LESSON XXI.

RESTRAINTS ON BUYING AND SELLING.

I MENTIONED that there were various ways in which the Government or the laws of a country give special assistance to certain industries, and that these privileges are accorded on the plea that the public good is served by that restraint on the freedom of others which the grant of a privilege always implies. It is probably for the good of the people at large that the right of practicing medicine is confined to those who have obtained a certificate of proficiency, and that the rule which holds good in physic might be extended with advantage to other callings. At present, however, these restrictions on freedom of industry are rather lessened than increased in number.

A hundred years ago, there was hardly a single calling, with the exception of farm labor, which any person could enter on without having been an apprentice, and sometimes without becoming the member of a trade company. There are parts of Europe—as for example in Southwestern Germany—where such a rule holds to the present day. It appears that the custom is not a good one, and that such privileged labor is apt to become very incompetent, and lacking in enterprise.

Similarly, there is no country in the world, except

England, where other people have the right of buying and selling to the best advantage, that is, without any artificial restrictions. If an Englishman wishes to buy a coat or a pair of shoes, he has the right to purchase either a London, or a country, or a foreign article at his pleasure. In other countries, however, it is the general rule that either the people are wholly forbidden to buy from foreigners, or are obliged to pay a heavy tax if they still have so good an opinion of foreign goods that they will have them, even at the increased price.*

Now it is quite clear that when such a hindrance is put on the person who wishes to supply himself with what he wants, a loss is put on him. If the customer's

* It must be said, however, in regard to this view, that a good many people in America and Europe, believe that it is of considerable advantage to the community to oblige buyers to get their goods from their immediate neighbors, rather than from the foreign manufacturers.

They claim that while the buyer for the moment pays more for the goods, the community to which he belongs is benefited by having the articles manufactured and used at home, and that the general welfare must be considered, rather than that of the individual buyer.

The question is a very complicated one, and cannot be discussed here. Those who believe that buying and selling should be unrestricted by the Government, are called Free-traders. Those who claim that foreign goods should be taxed, so that as many articles as possible should be manufactured at home, are called Protectionists. The writer of this book is a Free-trader. At the present date, 1872, England is the only country whose Government has adopted in full what are called Free-trade principles. Holland and Belgium have adopted them in part, while France, Germany, Spain, Italy, and the United States have, by placing greater or smaller taxes upon foreign goods, followed the theories of the protectionists.—EDITOR.

own country could sell him articles as cheap and good as the foreign country can, there would be no need to put the restraint on him, and the restraint would not be put on him. No one in France would think of putting a tax on English wine, because England makes no wine which is as good as that which France makes. No Chinese would think of taxing English tea, no Australian of taxing English meat. Any restraint, then, which is put on a customer is a certain loss.

Again, it is clear that when the tax is first put on, it is a gain to the man who makes or, at least, to the man who has a stock of the articles. If any man could compel everybody in his neighborhood to deal at his shop, he would make a large profit, as long as there was no other shop to compete with him. For a time at least, then, this restraint is a gain to the dealer. But when people find out that great profits can be made out of any trade, they are eager to engage in it, and thus it constantly happens that the poorest and the least prosperous business is that which the law favors, by compelling the people to trade only in a narrow market.

The loss, then, always falls on the buyer, and after a time the gain does not remain with the seller. Some one always loses, and in the end no person gains. Why, then, should such a system be undertaken at all, and why should it be carried on, when its effects are found out?

Of course I do not take into account such cases as those in which men, having influence in a Government, knowingly put a loss on others in order to get a gain themselves. Such things have happened, and will happen again, as long as strong men are dishonest, and other men are weak or ignorant. Except for the fact that such acts have the form of law on their side, they are just as much robbery as though a man picked one's pocket in the street, or stole one's money from one's house.

But these laws or customs are defended on the ground that it is desirable to have all kinds of industry planted in a country. Now if the industry is necessary to the defence of a country, there is great force in this reasoning. But then, we may depend on it that, unless the Government is very much to blame, they will be undertaken. If they are not, it is just as absurd for the law to order the work of the nation, as it is for it to order the work of a particular person, or as it would be for any person to try to do every thing for himself—grow his own food, make his own clothes, build his own house, and fashion his own tools—because he does not like to depend on others for the better and cheaper supply of these articles. In short, it is to prefer savage to civilized life.

An industry which will pay on its own merits always springs up in a country as soon as the advantage of following it is found out, and this is quite soon enough. Further, any country has a great advantage over every other country in two ways. It can supply the same goods without the cost of carriage. The home laborer knows better than the foreigner does how much of the article, and what quality of the article, is wanted. Now to take to the industry before it can be supplied cheaper and better at home than it can be from abroad, is to waste one's industry.

When, however, the tax is laid on, and the industry has been forced to grow, just as tropical plants may be made to grow in an English hothouse, it may be the case that an alteration in the law will do mischief to those who have been induced to trust to the law. It is a very hard thing to get rid of a law which creates such interests as would not naturally exist. It is like stripping off the roof of a hothouse, and leaving the plants within it to struggle, if they can, against a climate to which they are unsuited. Fortunately, indeed, man is more able to accommodate himself to hardship than a hothouse plant is to frost; and moreover, no one industry is so wholly unlike others as to render it impossible for the workman to betake himself to another calling when the assistance the law gave his old labor is withdrawn.

Two great countries have latterly passed through terrible wars. In the one, the nation was victorious—if, indeed, there can be said to be a victory in a civil war. In the other, it was vanquished. Both incurred great debts, which it is necessary to pay. The one, in order to find money, put heavy taxes on foreign goods, believing that it would greatly assist home industry. The hope has been disappointed, for the home industry has been far from flourishing, and the foreign trade of the country, except in those articles which are not assisted, has been ruined.

The other country has incurred a debt almost as vast as that of the United States. It has borrowed money in order to pay the debt, and has therefore to pay interest on its loans. Its statesmen, though they have the example of the American Republic before them, seem bent on following a disastrous example. The consequence of such a plan is as certain as that of any natural law can be. It will ruin foreign trade, will inflict great losses on the people, and in the end be a gain to no one.

LESSON XXII.

PUBLIC CHARITIES.

THERE is yet another kind of industry to which society or the State grants assistance, or to which it allows the grant of assistance on the part of private benefactors. I have already told you of the aid which the State gives directly to those who are able to do a public service which is of great value, but which is not saleable. I am now about to tell you of that aid which the State allows other people to give, under the name of endowments or public charities. These endowments are portions of property, the income of which is devoted forever to certain public purposes.

Now there are two objections which can always be made to such gifts. One is, that it is not expedient to allow any kind of property to be taken always out of the market, particularly if such property is one which is by nature limited in quantity, such as land. There always should be strong proof shown that the end of such permission is very good, before any person is allowed, however excellent his motives may be, to bind all men afterwards not to bring a particular quantity of property into the market. Any interference with selling or buying needs a defence. But if a charity is to be perpetual, it is necessary to grant this restraint over some kinds of property.

Next, the gift of these charities, in case they are bestowed on those who earn money by teaching, or get money for learning that which they will turn to profitable account afterwards, always lowers the earnings of others who do not share in the charity. The same fact holds good in the case of ordinary wages, if any public charity gives aid to ordinary laborers.

The reason is the following: The payment of labor depends generally on the cost of rendering the laborer fit for his employment, and on the number of persons who seek for the employment. Now if some aid is given to a particular employment, the advantage of following it is greater than it is in others, and more persons press into it. If, moreover, the endowment is of such a character as to contain such prizes as give a show of chance or luck to it, the employment to which it is tied is always more attractive than one the rewards of which are merely uniform or every-day.

Now just this sort of result happens in the case of those endowments which are given in aid of teachers. Those who get them are esteemed fortunate, however deserving they may be. Hence there are many persons willing to undertake the calling of a teacher. Still the income of the charity is to be reckoned up with all the wages which teachers earn. But the recompense is very unequally divided. Some have their earnings increased by the aid of the charity; but others have their earnings diminished—that is, do not get so much as they would have got had there been no charity at all. If no person got any thing from the charity, the earnings of all who are not assisted would rise, and the earnings of all would be equal in the case of all who have the same power and skill.

5*

So it is with charities given in aid of other wages
What a man earns must be sufficient to maintain him in
health, to enable him to bring up children, to provide
against the risk of sickness, and the certainty of old age.
If the law informs him that in case he is unable to do
so, it will maintain his children, will keep and cure him
when sick, and provide him a home in old age, his
wages will fall, even though he never takes advantage
of the offer. From one point of view, poor-rates are
really paid by those laborers who come within the class
to whom poor-law relief is a help, because their wages
are lowered by the pledge of assistance.

If, again, children are educated at the cost of a charity,
the other rule which I have so often laid down comes
into operation. The cost of rearing and teaching labor
is lowered, and with it the wages are lowered. It is
true that the person who has gained the benefit of the
charity gets far more than he would get, if no persons
but such as are reared by the charity entered into the
employment. But those who are reared at private cost
got less than they would if the whole of those who enter
the employment were reared at private cost. You will,
of course, remember that when I am speaking in this
manner, I am thinking of such knowledge or skill as
commonly gets employment in consideration of its usefulness.

If, therefore, the consequence of a charity is that it
interferes to some extent with the market of property,
if it tends to lower wages, and is certain to make the
payment of those who are not assisted lower than would
have been the case had no assistance been given to any
one, what good are these charities at all?

There was, no doubt, a time in which the value of

education and learning was scarcely admitted at all. Had they been left to those who could afford to pursue them for their own sake, they would, perhaps, have never been cultivated at all, or probably would have been cultivated very rarely. In those days, an endowment in aid of learning was a real public good; it afforded leisure and the means of life to those who busied themselves with something which was very useful, but for which there was no market. Whatever may be said for these charities now, there was a time in which they had a great value.

But at all times there are special branches of learning which have a great value, and yet are not marketable. The endowment which is given to such kinds of learning is now doing that which, in old days, these charities did for every kind of learning. You can see what the benefit to society would be if a man could discover some new force or process which would greatly save human labor. If it were possible to find a man who could give labor to such a discovery, it would be money well laid out to give him the leisure for the purpose.

Much more can be said for those endowments which are given in aid of those who are taught. It is more easy to show how riches can be and are gathered, than to show how they can be fairly divided or distributed. Now it very often happens that young people have great gifts of natural power, great force of character, and great willingness to learn. Poverty, however, and the lack of means by which they can be trained till such time as their powers can be made mature, are great hindrances to the progress of those whom everybody would wish to see prospering.

Now these charities are or could be made a very

powerful means for selecting and training such young
people. A good system of education, and a wise management of these charities, would make the road easy
to many a diligent child; nor will a system of education be perfect till such a scheme is worked out.   Men
of science do not grudge the spending of money on
searching into all forms of Nature.   But no discovery
is more pleasing than that of good gifts of ability and
character in children, and no money is better laid out
than in forwarding such deserving persons.

LESSON XIII.

THE WORK OF GOVERNMENT.

By this time, I suppose, my readers will have found out that it is an error to imagine that work can be got without paying for it. There are, no doubt, some great services which are done to mankind, but for which no wages are ever paid. There are some persons, again, who devote themselves to works of charity and well-doing, who neither expect reward nor would accept it if it were offered them; and there are, moreover, many ways in which persons may be paid for their services, apart from the common mode in which men are rewarded for work. But the rule holds good, that in some way or another most of those who work earn wages.

Now some of the most important work which can be done is performed by the Government of a country. It undertakes the defence of the whole people, either by police and courts of justice against those who break the peace or commit frauds at home, or by an army and navy against the passion of conquest in which States are sometimes apt to indulge. It controls education, gives relief to the destitute, and sits in judgment upon cases where people are likely to have a mistaken view of their own interests. Whether it always does what is best is a question; but it always does that which those who have the greatest power and influence think is best.

Again, it sometimes undertakes the management of a kind of work itself. Thus it always regulates the coins of the country, and frequently takes upon itself the business of issuing those pieces of paper which, as I mentioned in a former lesson, can, under certain circumstances and under certain rules, be made to act as money. So, again, in every civilized country, the Government undertakes the collection and distribution of letters. In many countries it does the same thing by the conveyance of persons and goods, for it takes railways in hand. Sometimes, as in England, it establishes banks for the poor. At times it lends money to persons who wish to improve property, or even to acquire property.

Now it is very easy to see why a Government undertakes some of these duties. We have already found out that human labor is always best bestowed when persons occupy themselves with some one business, and that to try a dozen things, unless under necessity, is to do the whole dozen ill. If, therefore, it would be a waste and an inconvenience for a man to undertake the defence of his own home, property, and person against domestic and foreign enemies, it is expedient to commit this office to some one else. But to whom could it be committed except to a Government which has the power to compel the strictest discipline, and if it be so disposed, can do the work in the best and the cheapest manner?

In short, a whole society may be compared to a vast factory, every one of the workmen in which is occupied in some industry for the general good. But it is necessary that over the whole of this huge partnership some management should be established, the officers of which should see that each man is allowed to do his work with the least possible hindrance and loss, that the whole of those who exercise their industry, should do so with the greatest possible safety; and that each person should feel that right will be done him, in case he thinks that wrong has been put upon him. The managers of this great partnership engage to maintain peace and order in the interests of all, and to check and control all whose conduct would throw the safe and constant working of the partnership out of gear.

It is not easy to say when a Government should take upon itself to hire laborers in order to perform industries which private persons or private partnerships can undertake. Three causes, however, may induce this kind of action. A Government may hire labor, and manufacture or perform a public service, either because it cannot trust ordinary traders; or because the work can be done at a cheaper rate by Government than it can by private enterprise; or because the necessary spirit of enterprise is wanting.

Unluckily, honesty bears a price. People are obliged to pay for that which only exists in limited quantity, and which it is at the same time very necessary to get. Now the habits of some persons, owing to the negligence of law, are so dishonest, that it is difficult to say whether you can trust their word at all when they pretend to sell genuine goods. Frauds and adulterations are part of the stock-in-trade of some men. But it is not difficult to see that a Government may be put to serious inconvenience, and a nation to great danger by the roguery of such tradesmen. Suppose this nation were forced to go to war, and found that the powder which it had bought was bad, because the manufacturer had cheated the nation, or that the preserved meat was unwholesome, or the bread made of bad flour, the country might be brought to the verge of ruin Cases of this kind have often happened, and in view of this danger, it may be, and it has often been, necessary for the Government to do this kind of work for itself.

In the second place, a Government dealing with a public service on the largest possible scale, may do the work more cheaply and effectually than any private company can.   A trade partnership could undertake the business of the Post Office, but it is very doubtful whether it would distribute letters with such cheapness, accuracy, and dispatch, as the Government does.

In the third place, the spirit of enterprise may be weak in a society.   The subscription of private capital has constructed English and American railways; but in every other country such works have been undertaken by Government, either in whole or in part.   And even in the United States, the great Pacific Railroad, completing the line across the Continent, was largely assisted by the Government.   So Government has made and maintained roads, erected public buildings, undertaken irrigation on a large scale, reclaimed waste land. Among an active and enterprising people such work would be superfluous or even mischievous, but when an important object has to be attained, it is not always wise for the State to wait till private persons take it in hand.

LESSON XXIV.

TAXES.

IF a Government does a service, it must, like every one else, be paid for doing it. It may possess an estate, the rents of which may be sufficient for meeting the charges to which it is put for performing the service which it undertakes. Sometimes this happens to a limited extent in this country. There are many ancient towns which possess large estates, the value of which has been greatly increased by the demand for building sites. But no general Government has ever had an estate sufficiently large to meet the expenses which are thought necessary for carrying on the various duties which a Government fulfils.

Recourse must therefore be had to some other source of income. The several persons who live in a community are called upon to contribute something out of their means towards the cost of a service which is a benefit to everybody: in other words, they pay taxes.

You will see at once why some taxes are put upon the inhabitants of certain places, and not on the whole nation. For example: suppose the land in any district of New Jersey were being washed away by the sea, as it is occasionally on the coast, and that by some outlay the waste of land might be stopped. In this case the people who live in Chicago should not be called on to pay towards saving the property of the people who possess land in those maritime counties : the necessary expenses should be met by a local rate.

Again, it is no doubt desirable in the minds of all who have any idea of what is the public good, that pauperism should be checked, and that crime should be detected and punished. To a certain extent both these social evils affect everybody : but they ought to affect the place where they occur most of all—pauperism almost entirely, crime to a great extent. It is the wise and just rule of our law that such a system should be adopted. The State aids the cost of pauperism a little, the cost of crime a great deal. The locality pays the greater part of the charges incurred for the first, and a considerable amount of the cost incurred for the second.

But, on the other hand, if the tax is devoted to purposes which benefit everybody, the tax should be collected from everybody, in so far as each person can pay it. The public defence is a matter of universal benefit. The invasion of an enemy may destroy the property of the wealthy, it is sure to stop the industry of the poor, who suffer even more than the rich by the miseries of war. Let us suppose, again, that part of the work of Government consists in rewarding those who have done some special benefit to their fellow-countrymen. Here also the whole nation should pay for that by which the whole nation is benefited.

There is then, apart from another consideration, which I shall refer to presently, a great propriety in distinguishing between taxes which are paid by the inhabitants of particular regions, and which are called local, and taxes which are paid by the whole community, because they are employed for purposes which are called imperial, or national. The distinction is founded on the fact, that people pay taxes in order to obtain some real or supposed benefit.

The other consideration, which could not, except for the last-named reason, be of very great weight, but which, taken with that reason, is of great value, is that the local collection and expenditure of taxes promotes saving and educates people to carry on the government under which they live, and to understand its working. If all the taxes needed for public purposes in the United States were paid into one vast treasury, and spent by some board or boards situated in Washington, there would certainly be great waste, and everybody but those who managed matters in these boards would be untrained in public business. Now no country has ever yet succeeded in obtaining real freedom where there has been no local Government, but where every thing has been done by the central Government.

The benefit of protection is general, and the cost ought as far as possible to be met by payments from all. At first sight it would seem as though women and children were more protected than strong men are. In a sense, perhaps, they are. But a little inquiry will show that everybody is so much protected by a good and wise Government, that the difference between the help given to one and to another is not worth reckoning. The effect of insecurity is to take away strength from all industry, enjoyment from all property. If society were at the mercy of violence, the strongest man would be only a little more helpful than a child.

Of course, it is the business of a Government to

make the cost as light as possible. Every tax that a person pays is so much taken away from his power of enjoyment, and every man has a natural right to enjoy the fruits of his labor. At any rate, it is clear that if the right of such an enjoyment were denied him, he would be in the condition of a slave, and as we have already seen, a slave has only the lowest motives for exertion, and no motives for improvement.

All cost is so much taken away from enjoyment. It cost far more labor to our forefathers to get the necessaries and comforts of life than it costs us, and as a consequence their enjoyments were fewer. It is impossible for labor to be carried on without cost, but the ingenuity of man is always directed towards making the cost as light as can be. So it is impossible for Government to be carried on without taxes, but it is the duty of Government to make the taxes as few as possible, and such as distress the people who pay them, as little as possible.

I have compared society to a great partnership in which the government are the managers. You will see from what I have already said in this lesson, that the comparison is made more clear by the way in which taxes are collected, and by the principle which ought to guide those who put taxes on the people. To take a tax for some purpose which does -not benefit all who are in the partnership, would be a wrong; to lay more taxes on the people than are sufficient to manage the great partnership, would be a waste—would be to pay one kind of labor more than its due. But it is plainly out of the question to imagine that the management could be carried on without cost or expense. All good service must be paid for, and wise government is the best of service.

LESSON XXV.

WHAT DO TAXES COME FROM?

EVERYBODY who gets the aid of Government should bear a portion of its expenses. But it is plain that those who have nothing cannot pay. A person who is maintained at the public charge, without being able to do any work in return for his maintenance, can pay nothing except in so far as those who maintain him pay taxes on his behalf. So those who can earn nothing, but are maintained from private sources, pay to the needs of the State only through their relatives and friends.

Now this very plain fact leads us to a very important rule. The only source from which a person can pay a tax, is from that portion of his earnings which is over and above the cost of his own subsistence, and the cost of those whom he must maintain by his labor. In our country it is seldom the case that the earnings of people leave them nothing whatever to pay in taxes. Some people allow themselves to pay a great deal more than they ought to pay, if they considered the true needs of themselves and their children. But it is rarely the case that a man's income is wholly consumed in bare necessaries, and that he has nothing left for enjoyment. Such men, then, can and do pay taxes; it may be very little but they generally pay something.

Some taxes are paid of a man's own free will—*i.c.*, he can avoid paying them if he chooses. No man need drink beer, wine, or spirits, or smoke tobacco against his will; and it is certain that he can contrive to live without the use of any of these. In the same way, tea and coffee are not absolute necessaries of life, though they have become such very familiar comforts that they may be almost called necessaries. Sugar, on the other hand, is a necessary of life; it is a kind of food, and a very important kind of food too. Now these articles are nearly the only objects on the use of which the Government of this country lays any taxes.

Some taxes, however, are paid whether a man wills or not. Most local taxes, poor-rates, house-tax, and the like are of this kind. So is a tax on a man's earnings, or his property, taken from the annual income of the former, or on the value of the latter. Such also are taxes levied on business, as on buying and selling. It is impossible to carry on the affairs of life without buying and selling.

Generally, however, small houses, low earnings, and little business dealings are not taxed. Perhaps the reason is that it would cost too much to collect them; perhaps it is seen that they would tend to cripple business, perhaps it is allowed that there is a class of persons who should not be made liable to pay taxes which they cannot avoid, because they have little more than enough to live on.

It will be clear, then, that if all taxes were put upon the earnings of people, and none on their spendings, the tax would be much heavier in the case of a man who has a family of children to keep, than it would be on one who has none; and would be much heavier also in the case of a man who cannot earn his income without great outgoings, than in that of a man whose income comes to him without any outlay whatever. A man who can choose his own expenses, and who is constrained to meet certain regular demands on him, may keep within compass. But if his expenses are fixed by some other will than his own, as would be the case if the taxes he pays were laid on his earnings and not on his spendings, it may very well happen that the tax he pays may press severely on his means.

Again, it will be clear that the tax which is paid by a man of small earnings, is felt to be harder than a far larger tax paid by a man of large earnings or large income, if it be the case that the poorer man is unable to avoid the tax. The sacrifice which poverty makes is far greater than that which wealth makes, just as the charity of the poor is greater self-denial than the gifts of the rich. A tax of fifty cents a week out of five dollars earnings, is a much more serious affair than taxes of five dollars a week out of an income of five thousand dollars a year. And when the wealth of the taxpayer is still greater, the sacrifice is still less.

Men whose incomes are very little may, however, pay a very large part of the taxes of a country; for though the earnings of each may be small, they become when added up a vast sum. The same rule holds good in their spendings. It has been reckoned that half the taxes of England are paid by people whose earnings are under ten dollars a week. They would, no doubt, be vastly better off if they saved a portion of that which they spend; but the amount which they do spend in tax-paying articles of their own free choice, is so great, that if it were saved, it would keep half the work of the

country going on. So vast is this amount, that it is hard
to say what would be done, if the money received by
the Government from this quarter were to cease pour-
ing in. But it is certain that more than half the misery,
poverty and crime which disgrace this country—and a
good many other countries too—would be arrested, if
people forbore to spend on those articles from which
the Government gets so much by taxation.

Sometimes a country does not take all that it needs
by taxes, but borrows money, and pays interest on that
which it has borrowed. The reason why this is done—
if the true reason is given—is that when a time of great
difficulty arises, it would be next to impossible to get
what is needed by ordinary taxation. It would be better to do so, but as long as the art of putting taxes on
is in so imperfect a state, a great increase in the expenses
of the Government would press with the greatest severity on the poorer classes—that is, on those whose earnings very little exceed their expenses.

Most countries have borrowed great sums of money,
and require a great income in annual taxes to pay the
charge for these loans. These sums have not always
been borrowed for the wisest purposes. Perhaps as
time goes on, and nations get to be wiser, and rulers get
wiser also, the disposition to enter upon projects which
require wasteful borrowing will be a great deal checked.
It is to be hoped that it will be; for there is no doubt
that in the long run, a country which has no debts, and
therefore comparatively slight taxes, will win in the race
against others which have incurred debts, and have
therefore put on heavy taxes.

THE PUNISHMENT OF CRIME.

WHY do men punish crime ? Why are some offences chastised by law, while others which are often very mischievous in their consequences, are either visited by light punishments, or not punished at all?

A crime is an offence against one individual or more, or against all individuals—*i.e.*, against the community at large. To the former class belong acts of violence or fraud committed on any person or persons; to the latter, acts which offend against society itself. Now there is a constant tendency to treat offences against persons as being offences against society, and to neglect to compensate the person who has undergone harm and loss, in the anxiety to chastise an offence which may be said to injure all men who live in the same community. Nay, the usages of modern law go further still; and Governments engage by treaty to give up persons who have committed crimes in their own country, and have fled to a foreign country in order to escape detection and punishment.

In early times the law took notice only of the injured person, and made it its business to assist or recompense him against a wrong-doer. In the oldest systems of European law, wrongs done to persons were

6

looked on as debts incurred, and when the injury was proved, the judge directed the wrong-doer to pay a sum of money to the wronged person; or in case he could not pay, adjudged him to be the slave of such a person. Even murder was punished with a heavy fine only. And to carry this notion out most fully, the quantity of the fine varied with the rank of the person against whom the crime was committed.

In course of time, however, another opinion began to prevail. It was seen that an offence, committed maliciously, was not only a wrong on the person injured, but a wrong to society itself. So important is the maintenance of order, and so serious are the consequences of disorder, that it was plainly the duty of Government to save society from these outrages. Thus if a man commits a forgery, though this is really an attempt to cheat some individual only, it was felt that this offence was so mischievous to credit and good faith—which are the bonds of society—that the punishment of the offence must be referred to Government only. Again, no grosser wrong can be conceived than wilful murder. But for many a year the law has ceased to trouble itself with the injury done to the family and friends of the murdered person, in its anxiety to avenge the wrong done to the order and security of society.

As nations become more civilized, this tendency to look on offences from a social, rather than from a personal point of view, grows stronger, and offences are constantly treated as crimes rather than as wrongs. Of course there are and always will be a number of cases in which the injury done to the individual is the only thing to be considered, and the only thing to be righted. Thus the carelessness which makes men suffer by a railway accident, is treated as a wrong which requires compensation. A theft of property is treated as a wrong against society; but a damage done to property is generally looked on solely as an injury to the person whose property has been diminished in value.

Some offences may be treated either as wrongs or crimes. If a man libels another—that is, says something of him which, being false and malicious, will injure him in his character or his calling—the person who is wronged may either try to get what are called damages for the injury, or may treat the person as a criminal, and try to get him punished. Violence done to a man's body may be chastised similarly in either way. The law has not yet declared, in these cases, that the mischief done to society is greater than that done to the person who has been the subject of the violence.

So much for the person injured. The offender, as soon as it has been decided that the deed is to be treated as a crime against society, is always visited with a heavier penalty than his offence could have possibly brought him gain. The reason is clear. It is the business of law, not only to right wrongs, but to frighten offenders. Now the wrong is not merely loss of property, even when the individual injured is alone considered. If a man robs his fellow-man of five dollars, it will not be a sufficient penalty to make him pay back the five dollars, for this is not the extent of the injury. He has abused trust, or put another in fear, or to pain. Besides, to merely give back the precise amount of the loss, would be to treat the wrong-doer as though he were only a debtor. Now an involuntary creditor—one who has been made a creditor against his will—may fairly claim more recompense than one who entered into an engagement with another of his free choice.

But, as we have seen, he has not only put the injured person to a loss, but all society. He has rendered necessary the maintenance of a police, of courts of justice, and prisons. Were there not such persons as he, all these costly arrangements need not be made. His conduct is not only a loss to society, but is a disgrace. It is to be regretted that no way has been found out by which those who commit crimes on the greatest scale— those who sacrifice people to warlike ambition—can be punished according to their deserts. Unfortunately, however, these great offences go unpunished.

Under these circumstances, then, those offenders whom the law does reach, are liable to pay what I may call a multiplied or a double penalty. The penalty is multiplied, because the offence is not to be reckoned only by the direct loss which the wrong has caused to the injured person. It is doubled, because not only the man who is the object of the offence is to be considered, but the security of society has to be taken into account too, and the costs to which society is put for the prosecution, correction, and punishment of crime.

But there is even another reason why society should seek to deter offenders. When a man is wronged by no fault of his own, he is not protected as he should be by that Government which guarantees his protection, and for whose guarantee he pays his part towards the expenses of state. To be obliged to defend a right, is to assert that wrong has been done. If it be proved that wrong has been done, it is the duty of the State to make the wrong good, if possible, or least to prevent its occurring again. From these motives, it sometimes happens that when certain crimes are committed, the law not only strives to seek out and punish the guilty persons, but puts a fine on the region where the crime was committed in order that the injured person may be righted, and the criminal be discovered.

LESSON XXVII.

THE PRINCIPLE OF PUNISHMENT.

As regards the offender, then, the first motive which influences the law in chastising him, is vengeance and security. To avenge a wrong is a natural impulse; to commit the duty of exercising this vengeance to the law, is to put it into the hands of a judge who can give sentence without passion, in accordance with a rule which has been laid down before the offence was committed. Nowadays, no one thinks of passing a law in order to punish an offence committed before the law existed. And it is moreover clear that the law intends by its punishments to afford security. It may, indeed, err in its anxiety to obtain this security, and its punishments may have, and have had, exactly the opposite result that was intended, for excessive severity defeats its own purpose.

But it has been held that the duty of the law is of a higher kind, and that along with the punishment, it ought to try to reform the criminal. Now there is no doubt that if it can do this, it may sometimes effect a great saving. Of all wasteful persons, there is none more wasteful than one who is constantly leading a life of crime. He is most wasteful if he is not detected and punished; but he is only a little less wasteful if he is.

Still there are limits to the benevolence which seeks to reform bad people at the expense of the State—that is, of those who pay taxes.

Most people, perhaps nearly all people, are agreed that we should try to reform young criminals.   There are two reasons for this.   In the first place, it may be fairly said that when very young people take to bad ways, it is not quite their own fault that they do so.   In ninety-nine cases out of a hundred they have had careless or bad parents.   Now it is not just to punish a child for his parents' fault.   It used to be thought just to do so, in barbarous times, but we have arrived at exactly opposite views on the subject in our days, and have even, perhaps, gone a little beyond what might be demanded, in order to avoid the older and barbarous rule. In the next place, there is sure to be a terrible loss incurred when a habit of crime begins in childhood.

It is more doubtful whether the same kind of care should be shown in the case of older culprits, especially when they happen to be persons who, having had a chance given them, have repeatedly offended.   It seems hard, when there is a great amount of undeserved suffering in the world, that the resources of society should be turned to the benefit of those who have brought upon themselves whatever inconvenience they suffer.   If anybody is to be helped, it surely seems that help is due to the deserving rather than to the undeserving.

There is yet another reason for the prevention and correction of offences.   It is a better motive than that of vengeance, and even than that of affording security to good order.   The crimes of bad men are a loss to society.   But they are also a disgrace to it.   Now there is nothing done by man which cannot be prevented by man, if it be only possible to find out the way in which the prevention may take effect. Probably there are many persons who never commit an offence against law in their whole lives, but who owe their freedom from bad actions to the fact that they are checked by a healthy fear of losing their character or reputation. Now it may be that there is not much hope for those whose character is lost already, and it may be the fact that very few of those who take to dishonest courses ever mend their ways. But it would be a great thing done if the evil were bounded by the present generation.

The good or ill conduct of a man is a matter of great interest to their fellow-men. It is a great mistake for anybody to think that he should be merely busied with his own conduct, and that he need be under no concern for that of others. It is true that he may not discover the exact amount of social mischief which crime and vice cause, but he may be certain that mischief is caused, and that his business is to check it.

It is easy to see the fact on a small scale in the management of a school. Perhaps order, obedience to lawful commands, regularity, good manners, mutual kindliness, care not to wantonly hurt each other's feelings, truthfulness, and similar acts of good conduct, are quite as important matters of education as the school learning which a boy picks up from his master and in his class. Every boy in school can understand the mischief which idle, disorderly, rude, and ill-mannered boys do to its discipline and success. Now no less mischief is done to society at large by these and similar vices, than is done to a school. They are not the less real, because they are not seen so plainly.

And this leads me to the last question which I raised

when I referred to the fact that many serious offences are visited with light penalties, or are not punished at all.

If a man tells a lie in a court of justice, when giving evidence, he commits an offence which is severely punished. If he tells a lie when he is selling something in his shop—as, for example, if he says that a particular article is genuine, when it is really adulterated, or that he gives a certain measure of any thing when the quantity is much below the measure—he is not punished at all, or punished very lightly. But he may do as much mischief to society by the trade lie as he does by false swearing.

So, again, if a man attacks another savagely in the street, or starves his children in order to gratify a base liking for drink, he very often gets off easily, or is not corrected at all; whereas, if he caused a riot, in which far less real mischief is done than in the other cases, he is treated—and justly treated—with great severity.

Now there is no doubt that the reason why this negligence occurs is frequently due to the fact, that the law does not take notice of many offences which it could and should chastise. But it is still more due to the fact, that it is desirable to limit the operation of law as much as is possible, due regard being had to the security and order of society, and to trust as much as possible to the judgment of what may be called public conscience or public opinion. If the disgrace which should attach to those who commit offences against what society knows to be right, were strong enough to deter all from evil practices, there would be no need for law or justice. As it is, law trusts much to this influence, and in time may perhaps trust more.

6*

LESSON XXVIII.

RESTRAINTS ON FREEDOM.

IF a man has any right, it is that of a free control over his own words, acts, and property. All that has been done for mankind, either in assisting it in getting its work done more easily, or in making life more safe and happy, has been done by the activity of free minds. Slavery makes no progress, as I have said before. Nor has there ever been any thing done for the moral good of man, except by those who, of their own free will, have considered their neighbors' good in the first place, and have thought very little of their own profit or advantage. They who have made men wiser and better have always made great sacrifices in order to do so: for there is no exercise of one's own will or freedom, which is more marked than that of the man who chooses what is right for its own sake, and cares nothing for the consequences.

But it cannot be denied that freedom is of necessity limited in a variety of ways. In the first place, no person can claim that his freedom should extend to allowing him to interfere with the freedom of others. There ought not to be—and properly speaking there cannot be—any right in another man's wrong. If it can be shown that what a man says is his, cannot be his without causing loss or misery to his neighbor, it should not be his for a moment after such a loss or misery is proved to come from the possession of a miscalled right. One of the most manifest of rights is that of property in that which is the result of one's own labor, or which has been purchased by one's own labor. But if there were a man in a besieged city, or to take a better instance still, on a desert island, who possessed by right of property all the food in the city, or all the food which had been saved from the wreck of the ship, and he would not allow any of them who were with him to share in any of that which is his, it is plain that in neither case would his companions allow him to exercise his full rights of property. In other words, they would not permit him to maintain a right, the full exercise of which would cause the direst misery to his neighbors.

What is true in the case I have quoted, holds good in other cases. Strict right is very often grievous wrong, and cannot be endured. This may be shown in many ways. It would seem to be a right that a man should be able to carry on what industry he pleases on his own premises. But if he carries on some trade which injures the health or destroys the comfort of others, his rights will be restrained. If a man possessing a vast estate were to pull down every house on it, forbid its cultivation, and seek to make it a desert, his claim to do what he wills with his own should be, and probably would be, resisted, even if he were not proved to be mad.

It is true that there is generally little necessity for checking the undue use of such a right as that which has been referred to just now, for no one, we should think, but a madman, would destroy his own property. But acts may be done on a small scale which society would

not perm.t on a large scale.   It is a difficulty to decide
when they are done on so large a scale as to call for the
interference of law.   When they are so done, the Legis-
lature sometimes deals with the difficulty.

Again, the rights of a parent over a child are necessary, in order that a home should be well governed.
But the law will not allow a father to ill-use his children,
to deny them the necessaries of life, and to refuse them
proper education.   The freedom or discretion of the
parent may be granted, but this freedom must have its
limits.   The same rules apply to other relations—as of
husband and wife, master and servant, teacher and
pupil.

The best state of society is that in which the greatest
possible liberty is given consistently with no wrong
being done to others.   In so far as this result can be
secured by law, the statesman makes it his business to
decide where liberty can be allowed, and where order
must be maintained.   He is, as it were, a judge between
those who claim a right, and those who assert that the
exercise of the right is a wrong.

But there are a number of instances in which the
liberty of the individual is in a manner restrained,
though no harm could accrue to society at large if he
used his liberty.   Thus, for example, there are certain
demands which fashion, or custom, or manners make upon
every person.   Most Americans wear the same fashion of
clothes, adopt the same customs, and accept or obey
certain rules of politeness or good manners.   No real
harm would happen if some persons thought proper to
wear their clothes inside out, or adopt a dress which
would be quite different from what is usual, or followed
out-of-the-way customs, or practised manners different

from what most people think proper behavior. Nations vary much in these particulars, and what would be right conduct in some countries, would be considered very strange and, perhaps, improper in this. Why should such restraints be put on the freedom of people?

The fact is that the usages and customs of life are part of that training by which people get the most difficult of all accomplishments—the habit of self-restraint or self-control. It does not follow that this habit is peculiar to civilized people only. There are savage or half-savage races who are most carefully polite and self-restrained. This is peculiarly the character of the Red Indian tribes of North America, who are nevertheless so uncivilized, in the full sense of the word, that they seem to be incapable of adopting a settled life.

That man or boy is not very likely to be worth much to the society in which he lives, who has no respect for the good opinion of others, or who is indifferent to their just censure. A proper sense of shame at misconduct or any breach of good manners, is the means by which men arrive at the best social gift they can obtain—a nice and careful sense of honor. The self-respect which every one ought to feel, and which is the foundation of true manliness in men and true grace in women, comes from the feeling that one has done nothing to forfeit the respect of those about one. But to get the respect of others, one must show respect to them—and give as well as take. Now, though this is giving up part of one's own will or liberty, it sacrifices a little in order to gain much more

LESSON XXIX.

THERE are certain callings which any man may enter on, if he is able to take them in hand, and can get his living by them. There are some which can be entered on only when the law allows the man to follow the occupation. There are some which every man is allowed to follow, but in the exercise of which the law puts a man under control. There are some in which the law only allows a limited number of persons to be engaged.

Now at the present time, whatever may have happened in time past, it is always supposed that any restraint put on those who have to choose the means by which to get their living, is put for the general good of the whole community, and that reason should be shown that this good is intended. In other words, freedom of occupation in the rule, restraint is the exception. But at different times in the history of all countries, the various kinds of restraint mentioned at the head of this lesson have applied to very different callings. Rulers have had very different views as to what is the public good. But some occupations have always been put under restraint, or the rule of a police.

The great majority of callings can be followed at pleasure. Any man may become a tradesman in the ordinary meaning of the word, or a common laborer, or a farmer. There never was, and indeed never could be a time, when men were prevented from occupying and tilling land, for the very good reason, that the means by which everybody lives must be obtained by agriculture and similar callings. There have been times indeed when persons who were engaged in tilling the soil were forbidden to go into any other calling, partly that the land might be tilled, partly, I fear, in order that laborers might be plentiful, and therefore labor be cheap.

But in old days a man could very seldom open a shop, at least in a town, whenever he pleased. In the old English towns, as in the towns of other countries, the right to keep a shop was granted only on application, generally after a payment, and after the person had been entered into the books of some trading company. This rule, for example, used to be universal in London. You may see many handsome buildings in the city of London, which are called the halls of certain companies. In those buildings, now generally devoted to feasts, the several members of these companies used to meet, and admit persons to the principal privilege which the company possessed, which was that of being the only persons who were allowed to deal in the several articles from which the company took its name or title.

This rule has long passed away among Englishmen, and never was in force in the United States. Anybody may now set up any ordinary shop wherever he pleases, either in town or country, and no one can hinder him; but the liberty of trade which the English and American people possess is not granted in many other countries. In certain German towns, for example, a journeyman is obliged to wait for years before he can get the license to open a shop, set up a manufacture, or follow a trade.

After he has got the license, he is often tied down by a host of regulations, which are found very inconvenient and oppressive. There can be no doubt that much of the activity and industry which belong to this country are due to the general freedom which people enjoy in the choice of their calling or occupation.

There are some kinds of industry among ourselves which, although they are free to anybody to choose, cannot be entered on without some previous apprenticeship. At present there is no law which forbids any man from undertaking any kind of manual labor, though in old times no person could follow any trade or art without having been apprenticed to it; but this law has been disused or abandoned. There are, indeed, trades or callings in which some persons are always apprenticed before they are able to follow them. The rule is not, as I have said, a law, but a custom of the trade, enforced by some by-law or regulation which the workmen in that trade have made for themselves. It may be doubted whether such a restraint is likely to last much longer. When the law does not speak, custom is pretty sure to give way to liberty.

As you have learned already, the wages which people receive in any calling are regulated partly by the need which there is for the service which such persons can render, partly by the cost of making the workman fit for his calling, partly by the number of persons willing to be employed. When there is a little need for the service, and the cost for supplying the service is small, and the number of workmen is great, wages will be low. When different circumstances arise, wages are high. Now the desire to obtain what the workman makes lies in the mind of the man who needs his service, and the workman can, by himself, exercise no control or influence over such a desire or demand.

He can, however, bring his influence to bear on the other two factors—as arithmeticians say—in the calculation. He may make labor dear and scarce, by making the preparation of the laborer costly, or by limiting the number of people seeking employment. Now an apprenticeship effects both these ends. It is possible that the apprentice may learn the art in which he is to be instructed in a quarter of the time during which his apprenticeship lasts. If the time be prolonged, the effect is that his power of earning wages on his own account is put off. But this is just the same as making his preparation more costly than it would naturally be.

The same process makes the number of laborers fewer. In some of those callings where it is the custom that workmen should have been apprenticed, there is often another custom, that no master can take more than a limited number of apprentices. Here the quantity of labor is directly limited. But it is also limited whenever more time than is necessary is given towards making the workman fit for his calling, since whatever makes some kinds of labor costly, makes some kinds of laborers scarce.

LESSON XXX.

LAWS FIXING PRICES.

It has often been thought to be good for the public at large that there should be a rule which might fix the number of persons engaged in, or, at least, restrain an excessive number of persons from entering into, any one calling. But the difficulty is to fix the number which should be employed or could be employed, and to decide on the callings which should be put under regulation. Even if the number could be settled, and the callings could be decided on, it is to be feared that a great many abuses would occur. It might be an advantage to enter on such an occupation, and they who would be appointed to manage the system, as well as those who might profit by it, might enter into some dishonest bargain.

There is no way to avoid the risk of such dishonesty, except by fixing the price at which the service or work should be sold. But there are very few objects which can be treated in this manner. In those which are so treated, it is only possible to take a rough or general rule by which to fix the price. This rule may be made much more exact in some cases than it can be in others. But in every case, the person who is subjected to the rule must be liberally dealt with, that the price which is fixed may cover the risk of his business.

In the days of our forefathers, it was the custom to fix the price of bread by law. One of the earliest laws among the English statutes is that which fixed the price of bread. Of course, no one could fix the price of corn, for the value of food depends on its plenty or scarcity, and plenty or scarcity—at least in those countries which cannot or will not buy in other countries when food is scarce at home—depends wholly on the seasons. Hence in England, which depended entirely on itself for all the supplies of food which its people needed, there were great variations in the price of bread. In cheap years it was excessively plentiful, in dear years it sometimes mounted three or even four times above the usual price. Now we need hardly be told that if in our time a loaf, which usually in England costs sixpence, were to be worth two shillings, many people would starve.

Our forefathers, of course, could find no means by which to prevent these sudden changes. They tried one or two plans, but they only made matters worse by their efforts. But they could—or thought they could— fix the price at which the baker's service should be paid. So they made a law which declared that the price of a certain weight of bread should always follow the price of a certain measure of wheat. In the same spirit, and with the same intention, they ruled that a certain measure of beer should follow the price of a certain measure of malt. The regulations have been given up, because, in course of time, it was argued that all the real advantage which the law attempted to secure for the public, could be obtained by competition among bakers and brewers. It is not, however, perfectly clear that com petition does always make the cheapest price, or that competition acts at all in certain callings.

They among my readers who live in towns are probably aware that the price at which public carriages can be used is fixed by law. A London cabman, who is licensed to carry persons in the carriage which he drives, is obliged, unless he have some reasonable excuse to the contrary, to carry any person who claims his services, and to carry him at a fixed price. The reason why this price has been fixed is, that the driver may not demand an excessive charge from those who are in his carriage. It is plain, however, that the price at which he may be constrained to carry them ought to cover his own maintenance and other wages—the cost of keeping his horse or horses, or repairing his carriage—of some return for the original cost of both horses and carriage—or the risks which he runs that he may not be employed, and of any change which may be expected to take place in the price of the food on which his horse or horses live.

But there is a difference between fixing a price at which a man shall work, and obliging him to fix the price at which he will work, and giving public notice of it. It seems that the latter is the fairer course, and it has been adopted in the case which I have given. It is clearly just to the man who does the labor, and it is even better for those who use the service or convenience. If the law fixes the price, the person who is controlled by the law may be, and constantly is, induced to say that the law puts the price too low, and may appeal to the public for more than the law allows him. But if he fixes his own price, and is obliged to publish and keep to it, he cannot complain of unfairness, since it is his own will whether he chooses to work at the rate at at which he fixes his own labor.

There are certain kinds of services in which the law is bound to fix the price. If it gives or permits a sole right of doing a necessary service, its duty is to regulate the rate at which the service is to be done. For in order that men should be free to fix the rate of that which they offer for sale, they who may need to use what is sold ought to have the power of dealing where they like. There is no freedom of trade in a bargain where one is obliged to buy, and another, being the only person who is able to sell, is perfectly able to exact whatever price he likes.

Hence the law (or those to whom the law gives powers) fixes the highest price at which a railway shall carry passengers and goods. In reality, everybody must use the services of a railway, if he wishes to be carried conveniently from place to place, or to procure goods which have to be conveyed from a distance. It is true that if the railway directors fixed too high a price, they might check the use of that convenience which they supply. But they would only check that use which people can make if they please, not the use which must be made. They might put an end to journeys taken for pleasure, but those which must be undertaken for business would go on. Hence the law does not allow them the privilege of fixing and publishing whatever price they please to set, but decides what is the highest price which they can claim. For the reason which I have given before, this is no wrong—no interference with free exchange. Wherever one dealer has such an advantage over the other dealer as to be able to charge what may be called a famine price, the law may fairly interfere.

LESSON XXXI.

REGULATIONS ON PROFESSIONS.

IT was stated in a former lesson that, as a rule, people are allowed by the laws under which they live, to choose the calling in which they may get their living; and that the laws which grant this liberty, while in force in the United States from almost the beginning of its history, have only been very gradually passed in England, and do not hold good in many other countries. Even in England and with us there are certain callings in which the law does not allow persons to engage, whenever and however they like, but still maintains restrictions which were once general.

They who engage, for example, in the two professions of law and physic, are obliged under penalties—or disabilities which come to the same thing as penalties—to go through a course of training which in effect is just the same as that of apprenticeship to a trade or craft. A lawyer has to go through a regular course of study for his profession, and pass an examination before a committee of lawyers appointed for the purpose, before he can be admitted to what is called the Bar, or the association of lawyers of his State. And so a doctor or surgeon is obliged to get experience in some other doctor's or surgeon's business, to study at some public hospital, and also to pass an examination, before he is allowed to carry on business on his own account.

Again, there are certain persons whom the Government employs, and whom it pays, either in wnole or in part, and from whom it exacts a proof that they are competent to do what they undertake. Schoolmasters appointed in schools which are brought under the control of Government are required to satisfy certain officers of Government that they are fit to undertake the business of education, at least as far as their own knowledge is concerned. So persons who are employed to navigate the ships which belong to the nation are supposed to be put to the test of whether they know their business, and are able to prevent the ship from being lost.

Now it is easy to account for these last-named cases. If the nation employs labor, it has a right to know whether those who offer themselves for employment are fit to undertake that which they profess to do. In ordinary business, where the master's eye is everywhere, or ought to be everywhere, evidence supplied by others as to the fitness of those whom he hires may be useful, but is not necessary; for the master or employer may be able to exercise his own judgment, not only to decide whether the person who wishes to work for him is fit, in point of knowledge, but also whether he is fit in point of power to use the knowledge which he possesses.

The eye of the Government is not everywhere. Hence it is necessary to do the best which can be done —to find out as far as mere knowledge goes on the part of those who aspire to public employment, whether they are equal to the duties which they profess to be able to fulfil. Of course this is not every thing. It is one thing to know, another to use that which is known, and to turn it to the best account. There are some people who can manage to lay out the goods they have for sale in so clever a manner as to make, so to speak, five dollars worth of their own look as well as twenty-five dollars' worth of another man's. And in just the same way people with very inferior powers and accomplishments may make a far more skilful and showy use of them than others who are possessed of far greater learning or information.

But why should law interfere in order to supply proof that a lawyer or physician is able to do that which he professes to do? Why is it more the duty of the State to prove that the one sells good advice about such rights as people possess in property, and the other good advice about their health, than to prove that a shoemaker knows how to make good shoes and a tailor good clothes? Why undertake this duty, and not another duty, of providing that a grocer should know how to buy his sugar and cheese, a butcher buy good animals for meat?

In some shape or other, the law does provide a means for preventing the abuse of any trade or occupation. It supplies a police in case of fraud or adulteration— that is, of passing off articles as genuine or sound, when they are not so, of punishing those who sell bad or unwholesome provisions. It is the business of Government to protect, as far as possible, all those whom it is bound to care for against force or fraud, and it does so with more or less success, and more or less zeal.

There must be some special reason or reasons why the law exacts proof of skill in the case of the two professions which I have named. One of these refers directly to the public good, the other assists the same object in a less direct manner.

Most people are fair enough judges of what they buy. There are certain goods, the quality of which every one of any experience knows. Such goods are provisions. So, again, it is no very difficult matter to find out whether a pair of shoes is worth what has been paid for them, or whether a suit of clothes has been properly made of such materials as the price will warrant. If the purchaser has been deceived by the tradesman, he has been wronged, and ought to be righted; but after all, the loss or inconvenience is not so serious as to require that the trader should be prohibited from carrying on his calling; or to justify the law in exacting proof that he ought to show his fitness before he is allowed to pursue the calling.

But in the case of the lawyer or physician, ignorance might cause ruin or death. It is not enough that the persons who use the services of those who are employed in these professions may have a means provided them for being righted, in case their advisers have been so unskilful as to do them a great wrong; it seems proper that precautions should be adopted in order to prevent, as far as possible, unskilfulness itself.

The other reason is that there are callings in which it is expedient to strengthen the intelligence of those who practise them by appealing to their mutual honor. Schoolboys know that there are many acts which it would be almost impossible for a master to find out, but which would disgrace, or ought to disgrace, the whole school if they were committed. Now such acts, when the boys are worth anything, are prevented by the good sense, or *honor* of the boys themselves.

7

But a profession is thus far like a school. It can act together, and have a character of its own. There are many people who feel that if they disgrace their school or their profession, they **are in the highest** degree disgracing themselves

FORBIDDEN CALLINGS.

SOME kinds of callings are absolutely forbidden. They are treated as in themselves illegal or unlawful; illegal, when the necessities of the State forbid persons to engage in an occupation which is not in itself dishonest or vicious, unlawful when the calling cannot be entered on or practiced without doing some injury to society at large. I will try to illustrate what I have said.

It has been stated several times that no reasonable law will prohibit or even control those persons who choose to devote their labor to agriculture. The more wheat or other grain is grown in any country, the more cattle, sheep, and pigs are reared, the better is it for the people at large. If the labor of the husbandman is devoted toward producing luxuries, or comforts, such a person is adding to the enjoyments of the people.

Still there is one plant which the farmer in England and some other countries is forbidden to grow. This is tobacco. There is no reason in nature why a farmer should not cultivate tobacco, as well as turnips. But the English government collects a tax on tobacco, and this tax is so considerable, and adds so much to the price of the article, that a variety of restrictions or regulations must be put on its importation into the country. Now in order to save the revenue from a loss which might arise in case private persons grew this plant for their own use, or for sale, the cultivation of tobacco is forbidden by law, except under such circumstances as could not possibly diminish the amount of the tax which is collected.

I will take another case. There is no natural reason why private persons should not coin money. In ancient times they did so, though always after having obtained a license. There is not much more difficulty in stamping gold, silver, or copper coins, than there is in stamping metal buttons. If the money which such private persons issued were as good or as fine as that which the Government issues from the Mint, the public would be none the worse off, and some persons think it would be even better off.

The restraint which is laid on the practice of coining —by which I do not mean putting bad money into circulation, which is one of the basest and meanest crimes which can be committed, but by which I mean the manufacture of as good money as comes out of the Mint—is partly imposed for the sake of the Mint itself, partly for the sake of the public.

The price of everything in this country is measured by gold. We speak of dimes and cents, because these words are short or convenient ways of expressing fractions of a dollar. But a person who buys or sells any article for a dime, or a cent, really buys and sells for the tenth, or the one hundreth part of a dollar. Now if it be inconvenient to reckon in such fractions, it would be impossible to use such little bits of gold as would be worth what a cent represents, or even what a dime does. Some of such pieces would be so small as to be almost invisible, most of them would be constantly lost, and would very rapidly wear out. It is therefore the practice of this country, and of other countries, to use pieces of silver and bronze or copper to denote those fractions of a sovereign, or whatever else may be the measure of price.

If the Government issues these pieces of silver and copper, and pledges itself to take them back at the rate of ten dimes, or one hundred cents to a dollar, these coins will be worth what they profess to be, even though the amount of silver or copper contained in them may not be actually worth the tenth and one hundredth part of the piece of gold we call a dollar. Now during the time that such pieces are in circulation, the Government is making a profit on the difference between the real and the nominal value of the silver and copper coins. This profit is devoted to two objects. It covers, in the first place, the cost of coining gold, the Mint being enabled to do this at no charge whatever. It covers the cost of the wear of silver and copper coins; for however much worn silver coins are, the Government will exchange these coins for new coins of full weight. The action of the Mint, therefore, is that of doing a great public service at no cost to the public.*

* At the date when this is written (June, 1872) gold and silver coins are not in use in the United States. They were used until the breaking out of the war in 1861, when paper currency, which had before been used for nothing smaller than a dollar, was introduced for dimes, quarter dollars and half dollars. The credit of the Government having been depreciated by the risks and losses of the war, its paper "promises to pay" are not yet worth as much

If private persons were allowed to coin silver and copper at their own will, part of the advantage which the Mint gets and gives to the public would become a matter of private profit. Were private coining carried out on a large scale, the Mint would be obliged to put a tax on the people in order to cover its expenses, or to charge the public for coining its gold.

But there is a stronger reason for keeping the right of coining money in the hands of the Government. It is very difficult for any person to find out when gold and silver are mixed with inferior metals, unless the latter is mixed to a large amount. Unfortunately, when frauds cannot be found out, many people are ready to practise them, and there is good reason to believe that if freedom in coining were allowed, it would very soon become freedom for swindling.

There are certain occupations which are not only illegal but unlawful—*i.e.*, are so bad in themselves that they are not allowed at all. Thus, for example, English law forbids the establishment of gambling-houses. Now, in one sense, there is a kind of gambling which nobody can prevent. If a man engages to buy any goods on what is called speculation—that is, in the hope that he will hereafter get a better price for what he buys than could be got at present—he may be said to gamble, for he is risking his property on an uncertainty. But no

as gold and silver. Each year since the close of the war they have come a little nearer to the value of specie; and doubtless in the course of a year or two, they will again be taken equally with specie for the full amount of their nominal value. When this comes about, gold and silver coins now hoarded up, or withdrawn from the country, will reappear, and be used as far as is found convenient.—EDITOR.

law should ever interfere with this kind of speculation, partly because it is a necessary part of trade, partly because the practice does a real good, by bringing about a thrifty use of articles when they are dear, and a prudent use of them when they are cheap.

But the law interferes with gambling when no possible good can come to the public by the practice, and when it is probable or certain that clever persons will cheat less shrewd people by apparent fairness. No possible good can come to society by betting on the success of a particular horse in a race, while a great many worthless people live, and a great deal of dishonesty is practised in connection with such wagers. It is doubtful, indeed, whether it be wagering or drunkenness which is the most powerful cause of ruin or crime. Still there is a certain amount of openness in this kind of speculation. The case is far worse when certain parties set up a gaming-booth, the players at which must certainly lose, however fair the game may seem; or when some wager is laid on a conjuring trick, which the inexperienced cannot see through. On such practices as these the law lays penalties, not only because the public ought to be protected against cheats, but because it is a crime to cheat, and those who are cheated are tempted to dishonesty by their losses.

LESSON XXXIII.

CALLINGS WHICH ARE UNDER A POLICE.

THERE are certain occupations, again, entrance into which is free, or nearly free to anybody who chooses to engage in them, but in which the persons who follow the calling are brought under stricter regulation than those who are engaged in ordinary trades or professions, and are rendered liable to police regulations. Some of these restraints are imposed in the interests of the revenue, some in the interests of the public. Of those which are imposed in the interests of the public, some respect its safety or comfort, some its morals or conduct.

Of these occupations, the most notable instance or example is that of the persons who are engaged in the sale of fermented or intoxicating drinks. Such persons, before they can follow this calling, are obliged to get some evidence of their character. They are called on to pay a sum of money for permission to keep their shop open at all. They are compelled to close the place in which they carry on their business at certain hours of the night, and on Sundays during certain hours of the day. They are at all times liable to the visits of the police. If they break the rules under which they are allowed to carry on their trade, they may be disabled from carrying on their business at all, or in other words be refused their license. It will be seen, therefore, that such persons are restrained or controlled in a great many directions in which ordinary traders are free.

These restraints are imposed partly in order to assist the morals and health of the people; partly in order to prevent breaches of public order and crime. The police authority which is exercised over public-houses, was first established because it was thought to be a duty to keep people from some temptations to drunkenness But it is upheld quite as much because drunken people are apt to be violent, and becaue public-houses may be, and indeed often are, places where crimes are hatched. Of course, such a use of them applies only to a very limited number, but unless the same regulation were extended to all, it would be impossible to deal with the cases in which the abuse might occur. Similarly, as the vendors of unwholesome drinks do a great mischief, it seems natural that the public should be protected against frauds, the effects of which might be very baneful.

Again, there is another class of traders which is put under restraints nearly as strict as those laid on the keepers of public-houses. This trade is that of a pawnbroker. This sort of calling is, unfortunately, a very necessary one for the poor, whose fortunes are frequently so much depressed, that they are obliged to borrow small sums on the security of such property as they have. Hence it has been said that the pawnbroker may be called the poor man's banker. But the circumstances which make such a person useful to those whose means are very narrow, render the shop of a pawnbroker a very convenient place for the sale of stolen goods. The pledge which is deposited must not be sold for a given time, and hence if the article has been

stolen, and the pawnbroker is unsuspicious, still more
if he is tacitly in league with the thief, all trace of the
article may be lost for so long a time as, in a great many
cases, to defy detection.   For this reason this calling is
one which is brought considerably within police control,
the public good curtailing the freedom which trade
should generally enjoy.

Again, it is believed to be a necessary protection to
public morals that theatres and places of public amusement should be controlled.   What might be amusing
may easily become vicious, and may consequently do a
great deal of mischief.   There are a great many things
which had better not be talked about, and many more
which had better not be seen.   It may therefore be
right and proper that they who wish to talk about and
exhibit such things should be checked from doing so.

Some callings are regulated with a view to the public
safety.   No Government, unless it were wholly careless,
would allow a manufactory of gunpowder to be set up
in a crowded town, or indeed in any place but that in
which the least possible injury could be done by any
accident.   So with manufacturers of fireworks and of
similarly explosive articles.   Even the storing of gunpowder in a town is—or ought to be—forbidden, or at
least watched with great care.   They who are familiar
with danger get careless in taking proper precautions
against it.   It is said that half the terrible accidents in
coal-mines are the direct consequence of carelessness,
and that they would never have occurred if miners and
owners of collieries were only commonly prudent.

Lastly, there are certain callings on the product of
which the Government collects a tax.   It does so on all
fermented liquors which are manufactured for sale

Such, for example, are the trades of the brewer, the maltster, and the distiller. If there were no superintendence exercised over these callings, and they who engaged in them were allowed to return to the proper officers what they said they had produced, without any inquiry or scrutiny into the truth of their statements, it is very likely that some persons would state what was false. In such a case two wrongs are done. One of these is to the public at large, which has, by proper authority, imposed a tax on such and such articles, with a view to meet public expenses. The other is to the fair dealer, who having paid what is due on his own part, is trading against and along with a man who has taken an unfair advantage.

In countries in which a great number of foreign articles are taxed, the business of the unfair shipper— or, as he is called, the smuggler—is followed by many persons. As to many there seems to be no justice in the laws which Governments impose for the sake of preventing the use of foreign-made goods, very many people encourage the smuggler in his calling. Now that, however, a wiser notion of trade commences to prevail, the smuggler is considered but a vulgar cheat, who not only defrauds the Government, but will most likely defraud those who are foolish enough to have dealings with him.

LESSON XXXIV.

POOR-LAWS.

THEY who will not work for themselves have no right to live on the labor of others. To claim that they should so live, either wholly or partly, is to demand that the laws which govern society, and by which it subsists, should be suspended in their favor.

But that which they have no right to claim, society may be generous enough to grant, and that for very good reasons. In most countries the law allows no one to perish for want of the necessaries of life, if the destitute person make application to those who are appointed to the duty of relieving this distress; in other words, the relief of the poor, by means of a great public charity, is established by law. Of course the law intends that this charity should not be abused; that persons should not have the assistance unless they are really destitute; that it should be only of the necessaries of life, and that the relief should not be of such a character as to make people careless or improvident.

The laws of most civilized countries then, acknowledge that every living person has a right to the means of life. It is probable that the origin of this rule of our law was a sense of religious duty. But the custom is defended for other reasons. To see human misery, and to allow it to be unrelieved, is apt to harden the heart, to make men cruel. Now it is better that this relief should be given on system, rather than by the hand of private charity, which is often indiscreet, and must be partial. Besides, even where the relief of distress is very sparingly allowed by law, it is found necessary to check begging. Again, since the mass of those who obtain relief have passed or are passing a life of toil, and as it often happens that the wages received are not in proportion to the work which has been done, and its value, it is thought that they who have worked for others should live, partly at least, on the labor of others. Again, there are many misfortunes which no human fore-sight can prevent, and these, it is said, common humanity should constrain us to succor. It is moreover asserted that society is saved from risks of a very serious kind as long as destitute persons are not made desperate and therefore dangerous.

There is much force in these arguments. It is wor-thy of note that in those countries where distress is not relieved by law, another claim is set up—the right to work or employment. There are many who say that as long as people are willing to work, society or the State ought to find them occupation. But there is a great deal of difference between these two demands—every-body has a right to subsist: everybody has a right to work.

If you have read this little book to any advantage, you will have seen that by far the largest number of people in every country do work; that they work best when they choose for themselves that kind of labor for which they find themselves most fit, and that any attempt on the part of Government to parcel out work for each person is no very wise act. A man with a great estate, or a great business, often works very hard indeed—perhaps harder by far than any who labor for ordinary wages.

Now if this right to labor were maintained, everybody who is willing and able to work should be provided with his own special kind of industry. It is not sufficient only that that the carpenter, the mason, the compositor, the tailor, the shoemaker, the baker, and others who are occupied in manual employments, should be found work; but other persons must be equally cared for—the doctor ought to be supplied with patients, the lawyer with clients, the shopkeeper with customers, the teacher with pupils, the author with readers of his books. I do not think it will be difficult for you to see that such an undertaking would induce utter confusion—is, indeed, a manifest absurdity. It will be plain also, that under such circumstances, most of the motives which induce men to improve their work would be taken away.

If it be answered that they who make this proposal do not intend their rule to apply to any but certain kinds of labor, then it is plain that they are asking that certain workmen should live on the labor of other workmen, and that they are attempting to draw a line which cannot be drawn with fairness. For unless some principle be laid down which shall decide what kind of laborers must be provided with employment, all that the proposal means is that certain persons should be treated with favor at the expense of other persons.

There is one danger attending the law which relieves the destitute. I have already spoken of it, when I said that it may make people careless or improvident. To take away the motives to foresight and thrift is a serious evil, and there is no doubt that there have been times when assistance has been given so indiscreetly that working men have been degraded by it.

The only way in which this danger can be avoided is by making the acceptance of relief very irksome to those who receive it, while they are able to work, by raising up a wholesome feeling that it is disgraceful for strong men and women to get their living at the expense of other people, and only a little less disgraceful for persons not to provide, when they are strong and in full work, against the risks of sickness and want of employment. If working men had only common prudence and forethought, there would be very little real poverty in this country. Distress does not often come because there are too many workmen for the employment that might be got, but because the workman lives from hand to mouth.

Those poor persons are most to be pitied, and have the best title to public charity, who are not themselves to blame for the poverty in which they are placed. Such are the destitute and orphan children of the poor. Such are also a great many women, employment for whom is scanty and ill-paid. Perhaps in such cases the law might incline a little towards finding a field for labor. Now it is not always easy to find such labor at home; but there are many colonies and territories where women's labor is very scarce, and where children, who are just beginning to be able to work, would be taken and well cared for. It is not proper to send vicious or idle people to a newly-settled country, but such a country is just the place for those who are willing to work, and find little room for themselves at home.

LESSON XXXV.

THE PROTECTION OF THE WEAK.

WE are told that the existing races of animals have survived, or have been changed from ancient forms or life, because they have had certain advantages of form or structure, by which they have been enabled to live while other kinds have perished. This may be a very good account of the way in which most animals have successfully struggled for existence, but it does not correspond with the history of human civilization.

There have been times in which the strong habitually oppressed the weak; in which inferior races of men—that is, those nations which had less strength, or skill in war—have been enslaved and destroyed by superior or more powerful tribes, in which therefore the might of the strongest formed the rule of human life. But these practices prevailed in barbarous ages, and are justly condemned by good sense as well as by humanity.

As regards man, there is just so much truth in the theory, that certain races grow weaker or disappear before others. Thus the red man in America seems to be slowly perishing before the white. So does the black in Australia and the Maori in New Zealand. But there are other peoples which are able to exist and thrive, even when they are brought into contact with the most highly-civilized races, or are placed in the most unfavorable circumstances. Thus, the negro does not fail before the white man in Africa, his own home, or in those parts of the American continent to which he has been forcibly carried. Nor has there ever been any race which has been, one would have thought, so constantly within the risk of being destroyed by violence as the Jewish; but the Jews present one of the highest types of civilization and strength.

The more thoroughly men act on the principles of social science, and on the laws which govern society, the more tender are they of those who are weak and helpless. The reason is plain. The spirit of civilization is that of law, and the first business of law is to protect the weak against the strong—that is, to resist the operation of that tendency which has been said to have *selected* in course of time the races of animals which exist in the world. For the strength of social life consists in the helplessness of each man apart from his fellow-men. An individual in a civilized society strives, as I told you at first, to do one thing only in the best possible way. A savage is obliged to do every thing for himself. In order that the first may live in comfort, he should be surrounded by as many persons as can also live in comfort. In order that the savage may thrive and live in plenty, there should be as few persons as possible to share existence with him.

The willingness to protect the weak is no doubt, then, derived from a sense of self-interest. Insecurity affects everybody more or less, the mass of men most of all. Hence it is often necessary in a civilized country for those who are well-to-do to seek how they may better the condition of those who are badly off, because the neglect of such a course of action brings inconvenience or loss or evil to those who might be supposed to have no connection with the fortunes of others.

For example, if society were governed only by the interest of the strongest, and if it did not signify what became of the weak, provided that interest was served, there would be no necessity for the proper administration of justice. But the wealthiest person in a civilized community needs the protection of the law as much as, perhaps more than, an ordinary workman. His property, if it were not for the equal protection which the law affords, might be exposed to injury, rapine, or robbery from a thousand quarters. Unguarded by law, he is helpless in the extreme. Hence it has always happened in the history of the various steps by which we have gained our social and civil liberties, that the richest men have had to make common cause with the people.

Let us take another example. In times bygone nobody troubled himself, except so far as he was himself concerned, with the laws of health. Two centuries ago London was wasted by the plague, year after year. The cause was the great filthiness of the people. Since that time England has been visited with several diseases, which have been more or less deadly. In time people began to notice that the worst ravages of these disorders occurred in places where no attention was paid to cleanliness. At last it has been distinctly understood that there are very few complaints of an infectious kind which cannot be prevented by attention to certain rules, and that if persons would abide by these rules many plagues would disappear.

It is not enough, however, that this or that man

should regularly wash himself, wear clean linen, or other clothing, take care to live in a house which is kept pure, and provide himself with wholesome food and water; it is found to be of importance that his neighbor should do too. Hence the public health has come to be a matter of great consideration, and although much remains to be done before cleanliness is universal, there is a great difference between the present and the past. We have found out at last that the best way to keep one's self in safety is to better the condition of one's neighbor.

There is not a single law of nature which is contrary to or inconsistent with any other law. Take, if you choose, society, and consider the members of it as pursuing only their private interest, and you will find that they will pursue it best, if they follow exactly the course of action which duty would bid them adopt; that vice and loss are the same things; that virtue and gain correspond in the long run. In the same way it will be discovered that the laws of health are only another form of the laws of prudence and good sense; that what is foolish is wrong, and that what is wise is right.

But if this be the case, how is it that the world is so full of vice, crime, misery, poverty? It is because people are always preferring the present to the future, neglecting what conscience prompts and experience affirms, for the sake of some immediate temptation or pleasure. It is the faculty of man to remember in order that he may foresee. Nor can people begin the practice of foresight too young. At first they use the wise and affectionate experience of their elders. In time they find out that what was at first without meaning or reason to them is full of truth and order; and that if they please they can see and work with the truth and wisdom which they have learned.

LESSON XXXVL

EMIGRATION.

LET it be supposed that too many persons are living in any country to be comfortable, or even to subsist decently, either because some sudden scarcity has occurred, or because some dearth of employment has arisen. How far can such persons be put into a position to better themselves by emigrating to colonies or new settlements ?

There is one way in which a country may be relieved of an excess of inhabitants. A whole slice, so to speak, of the community may be taken—from the highest and richest personages down to the poorest and lowest— and this may be transplanted bodily to the new country. In such a scheme there must be some persons of all ranks, conditions and callings. But this means of relieving any community of an excess of persons has never been adopted in modern times; it used to be done anciently.

Now it is quite clear that society would be all the better if it could get rid of its worst people. At one time the Government of England used to carry out such a plan; but it has now abandoned it. It is plainly wrong to take or transport such persons to a place where other and honest people live. It is the same sort of thing as putting all one's refuse into another person's house. And even if no honest people lived in the settlement, it is a very serious or dangerous act to try to make a colony of the worst kind of people.

Next, it would be a good thing if all the idle people could go; but it would not be right to force them, and it is perfectly clear that they will not do so of their own accord. There is no room for idle people in a new settlement. They would find it difficult to get such enjoyments as are to be got in a country where there is a crowd, and where any one who spends is welcome. But it is clear that idle people, and those who follow callings which add nothing to wealth, or who exercise no profitable labor, are the plainest examples of an excess of persons. They do no real work, and they compete against others for the means of life. But it is also clear that the colonists would not care to have them.

Nor would those go who cannot work for their own living. This is another class of persons who are in excess. If there were no inmates of workhouses, it is plain that the country would be the better off; but no society would be better off by gaining those who are obliged to be inmates of workhouses, because they cannot get their own living. It is not easy to get rid of thieves, idlers, and paupers.

A colony is anxious to take those only who are willing to work, and able to work with advantage. Many people are willing to work, but unluckily their work is not wanted.

It will always, for instance, take agricultural laborers. The reason is clear: the natural industry of a colony is agriculture. A laborer who can do agricultural work in all its branches is always serviceable, but in a colony he is worth any pains to get. It is unfortunate for such laborers that they are usually so poor that they cannot get away; generally so ignorant of any thing but the work which they do so well, that they do not know how to better themselves. But there is no doubt that if they did leave this country it would be a gain to them. It would be no advantage to the country which they leave.

A handy artisan, like a carpenter or mason, and especially such an artisan as can do a number of things, is, after the agricultural laborer, the best sort of person to get on in a new settlement. His work is always wanted, he can get regular employment; and if, in addition to what he actually knows, he is also drilled so well in what I called in a former lesson the master-knowledge, that he can easily learn how to do other things, he is still more sure to succeed.

A jack-of-all-trades in a thickly-peopled country is not very likely to prosper; but a jack-of-all-trades in a new country, provided he be industrious and honest, has every chance of success.

Again, a person who is able to get his living in a thickly-peopled country, will very often find that there is no place for him in a new settlement. He may be honest, industrious, intelligent; but he may find no room for his work, his character, or his abilities. The reason for this is as follows :—

You have learned in former lessons how it is that in a country like our own, the division of employments is carried out to the fullest extent. It is discovered that the greatest quickness and power is attained, when each person does one thing, or a part of one thing. Now the greater the quickness and power, the greater is the cheapness; or, in other words, the more fully is the article on which the workman is employed, supplied for the wants of those who need it.

But in a new country no such rule holds. In course of time, no doubt, the same cause which brings about this division of employment will work in such countries. They will then become like such places as those which supply new-comers to new settlements; but till such a state of things takes place, the most useful persons are not those who can do a part of one thing, but those who can do the whole of a great many things; and thus the more completely persons are trained to do one thing, or the part of one thing only, the less fitted are they to become colonists in a new settlement.

Now what is the result of these facts? It is that old and fully-settled countries will be found to stand to these new countries in much the same position that the inhabitants of a town do to those of the country. Each does the other a great service. The town makes the comforts of life easier of attainment; the country supplies the necessaries of life more regularly and certainly. If men really understood their own interest and their own good, they would look on the whole civilized world as one country, the inhabitants of which are obliged to discover that they can gain their own ends best when they do most for the service and good of others.

THE END.

QUESTIONS OF THE DAY.

3

www.ingramcontent.com/pod-product-compliance
Lightning Source LLC
Chambersburg PA
CBHW020546270326
41927CB00006B/743